In Other Words

In
Other
by # Words
Marie Cardinal

Postscript by Annie Leclerc

TRANSLATED BY AMY COOPER

Indiana University Press

BLOOMINGTON AND INDIANAPOLIS

Library of Congress Cataloging-in-Publication Data

Cardinal, Marie.
    [Autrement dit. English]
    In other words / by Marie Cardinal ; postscript by Annie Leclerc ;
translated by Amy Cooper.
        p. cm.
    Includes conversations with A. Leclerc.
    Includes bibliographical references.
    ISBN 0-253-32929-9. — ISBN 0-253-20992-7 (pbk.)
    I. Leclerc, Annie, date. II. Title.
PQ2663.A7A9313 1995
848'.91403—dc20   95-8257

    1 2 3 4 5 00 99 98 97 96 95

Contents

FOREWORD BY CAROLYN A. DURHAM

"Some years ago, in 1983 I believe, I read Marie Cardinal's *The Words to Say It.* . . . It is a fascinating book." The prior reading experience that Toni Morrison recalls in the preface to her 1992 publication, *Playing in the Dark,* is one that America's most recent Nobel laureate shares with a great many other readers throughout the world. Marie Cardinal is among the best-known and most widely read of the current generation of francophone women writers. In the course of a career that now spans thirty years, she has produced fifteen works of fiction and autobiography, including three major novels since 1987 one of which, *Devotion and Disorder,* is already available in English translation. Yet *The Words to Say It,* the 1975 best-seller that established Cardinal as one of France's most popular writers, continues to attract new readers and to retain, as in the case of Morrison, its hold over their imaginations long after they have finished reading. This powerful and compelling account of the long-term psychoanalysis through which a woman struggles to emerge from years of madness originally sold over 320,000 copies in France, a country in which sales of thirty thousand are sufficient to qualify a book as a best-seller, and it was successfully adapted to the movie screen in 1983. There have been translations into eighteen languages, including the 1983 English version to which Morrison refers.

Statistics, however, can't really begin to convey adequately the importance of *The Words to Say It.* Cardinal's autobiographical novel is one of those very rare texts whose significance is demonstrated less by sales figures or even critical acclaim than by the role it has played in the actual lives of its readers, the direct action to which it has inspired them. Judging by the sheer volume of the correspondence that these readers, eighty percent of them women, subsequently addressed to Cardinal, and the efforts they made to encounter her in person, *The Words to Say It* stands with Betty Friedan's *The Feminine Mystique* (1963) and Simone de Beauvoir's *The Second Sex* (1949) as one of the most influential texts of contemporary feminism. *In Other Words* was born within this immediate context; it is Cardinal's generous effort to respond yet again to those who took seriously her commitment to the communicative function of language, to her call for both self-expression and for dialogue, to her belief that one can and should discover "the words to say it":

> I meet many people, as it happens (twenty-six meetings, debates, conferences, etc., in the past five months) and I receive thousands of letters. . . . [T]hese people tell me their names, their anxieties or their joys, they tell me their age, their work, very often they make an enormous effort to express themselves; and I, in exchange, send them a "Thank you, thank you, I'm very touched. . . . Sincerely yours, etc.," for fear of giving them too much of my time, of revealing my own ignorance, of claiming an importance for each one that I don't have, and that I don't want to have. Yet it is true that I'm touched, that I want to talk with them, want to exchange words, want to speak, don't really want to write. (1)

In some sense, then, one might describe *In Other Words* as both an occasional text and a kind of sequel to *The Words to Say It* in which Cardinal returns to a number of concerns originally raised in the earlier work and of particular interest to its readers. One can well imagine the anticipation and excitement with which this audience welcomed the publication in 1977 of *In Other Words,* a pleasure of discovery that Cardinal's many American readers will finally be able to share.

Appropriately, the context in which the book was

developed played a major role in determining its form and structure as well as its thematic content. To a large extent, *In Other Words* successfully reflects Cardinal's expressed desire to talk rather than to write: "The following pages are, therefore, often spoken pages" (2). The project was conceived from the beginning as collaborative; in part, it consists of the transcribed recordings of a series of conversations between Cardinal and Annie Leclerc, herself a well-known feminist novelist and essayist whose works—notably, *Parole de femme* (1974)—have been widely translated. Leclerc's 1977 essay, "Love Letter," originally published in *Coming to Writing,* a work written in collaboration with Hélène Cixous and Madeleine Gagnon, inspired "Annie Leclerc Writing A Letter with Vermeer," Jane Gallop's important and timely discussion of what she calls the problem of *écriture féminine* (154). Gallop's essay identifies and articulates the precise historical moment when it first became clear that American feminist criticism had begun to shift direction, in direct response to the influence of texts translated from the French, in order to explore its interests "not only in feminist social, political, and psychological issues, but also in 'writing'" (Gallop, 137).

The dialogue between Cardinal and Leclerc is also a "coming to writing" and an example of the power of translation, the capacity of some texts to "carry across" into others (etymologically, the word *translate* derives from *trans-,* across + *latus,* carried). The title of *In Other Words* not only refers back to the book's relationship to *The Words to Say It,* it also functions self-referentially to identify the interplay of two kinds of discourse included within the text itself. Despite Cardinal's initial conviction that she wants to address her readers through speech rather than writing, she quickly discovers that the inseparability of form and content includes a clear and insurmountable distinction between the spoken word and "these subjects [that] belonged to the world that I wanted to write about and that, moreover, I never stop writing about" (7). Thus, Cardinal's conversations with Leclerc are punctuated by a series of written intertexts, consisting, in particular, of memories of her childhood in Algeria and of speculative reflections on topics such as colonialism, the family, and writing itself. Moreover, what Annie Leclerc calls Marie's "domineering need to write; not to write what had been spoken, but to write these words that speech had touched and awakened, heavy, urgent, and obscure" gradually infects Annie as well: "At the same time, I told Marie of my desire to write a few pages of my own for this book" (174). Leclerc's "Postscript" concludes the text by a final echoing "in other words" of much of what has preceded.

As a whole, what results is a text that is difficult to describe and impossible to define or to classify. As Cardinal notes in an interview at the time of the book's release in France: "I haven't cheated. I have been honest. This book is not an essay, nor a novel, nor is it an interview. I wanted it to be different. If I had been able to, I would have included poetry. For no reason except to vary the genre. It's just too bad for purists" (my translation). The generic fluidity and the digressive and parenthetical structure that characterize *In Other Words* reflect what Leclerc identifies in Cardinal as a complementarity between the "vague" and the "rule bound": "During the course of our conversations, Annie often made me realize that all within me is a mix of uncertainty [*vague*] and rules. . . . it is true that I need rules. It is from these rules that I can wander [*divaguer*], and I don't know how to live if I don't wander" (16). Cardinal and Leclerc posit this constant and necessary tension between the desire to conform and the desire to subvert, between the need for rules and the need to break them, as not only characteristic of women in general but as common both to the lives they lead and to the texts they produce. Women's simultaneous and paradoxical immersion in the very cultural and literary system that they seek to oppose ac-

counts for the dual action of creation and destruction, of
ordering and resistance, that in part defines the specificity of female writing: "We must write. Trace our own text,
day after day. . . . Subvert, day after day, the other text that
prevents us" (182).

In an early link between French and Anglo-American feminist concerns (1981), Elizabeth Abel identified this
same textual practice as one primary objective of feminist
criticism: "Aware that women writers inevitably engage a
literary history and system of conventions shaped primarily
by men, feminist critics now often strive to elucidate the acts
of revision, appropriation, and subversion that constitute a
female text" (Abel, 174). Moreover, in keeping with the
dialectics of the vague and the rule bound, Cardinal's *In
Other Words* both illustrates the process by which women
writers defy traditional norms of form and genre and offers
us one of the very few examples available of what we might
identify as an original and specifically cross-cultural—indeed, Franco-Anglo-American—form or genre, that of the
"feminist essay." One of the most frequent objections to
notions of what is variously identified as an *écriture féminine*,
a female poetics, or a women's aesthetics has been the
failure of its theoreticians either to provide an adequate
definition or to cite specific and concrete examples of what
they mean by these terms. *In Other Words* joins a very
limited number of other essays—of which the most important include Virginia Woolf's *A Room of One's Own*, Rachel
Blau DuPlessis's "For the Etruscans," and Hélène Cixous's
"The Laugh of the Medusa"—that exemplify the writing
practice they simultaneously seek to define and theorize.
Together, these texts suggest that women's writing will be,
for example, intertexual, interdisciplinary, process-ori-
ented, collaborative, multivoiced, conversational, rhythmi-
cally fluid, digressive, fragmented, marked by repetition
and interruption, and self-reflexive.

Although *In Other Words* exhibits all of the above traits, there are two characteristics in particular of what I have called the feminist essay on which I want to focus more closely in this context. In the first place, Cardinal, like Woolf and DuPlessis, supports the view that such a text will be both experimental in form and grounded in material reality. Just as Woolf in *A Room of One's Own* systematically transforms fragmentation and interruptibility, which characterize the actual conditions of many women's lives and often impede their aesthetic productivity, into a brilliantly innovative narrative strategy, Cardinal's own texts provide a model for her similar conviction that women can and will use the structures and the vocabulary of their own domestic sphere to read and write their way into existence:

> For those who are against this evolution, which will be a revolution in reality, I only see one measure to take to prevent it: henceforth, prevent women from learning to read and write; in any way you can, keep them distanced from words. Leave them with only the language of the household to express themselves, give them the language of cooking and cleaning. And again . . . it's too late. They will find once more the way to exist, thanks to cooking, cutting, fermentation, birth, blood, guts, rot, dirt, water, air, meat, fish, egg, fever, vomit, song. And everything will start anew. . . . (134)

Cardinal's preoccupation with female literacy, a subject to which she returns repeatedly throughout *In Other Words,* also leads her to interpret women's writing as inherently collaborative. The individual writer simultaneously brings a common female world into existence and serves as an example that other women can follow. Thus Cardinal locates her particular talent as a writer not in the ability to express her own self but to discover within that self what she shares with other women: "In my books I think that readers meet a woman who lives in France today, and who basically resembles all women. That is who I am" (48). Similarly,

Cardinal's desire to "write for" those women who live within "the essential universe of women" but who don't "know how to express what they [have] understood" (52) has a double value. Not only do these women represent her ideal readers— "These women touch me; I wish they could read my books, and I swear that I think of them when I write" (51)—but they also implicitly collaborate in the production of work designed to speak their silence: "I want to write for them. I want to give them words that will be arms" (64). In this context, of course, *In Other Words* serves as a remarkably clear illustration of its own theory. As we have seen, collaboration characterizes the book as a whole, explicitly conceived as "a conversation with others." If, as Cardinal quickly points out, Annie Leclerc can hardly be submerged in "the anonymity of 'others'" (3), she too will nevertheless be transformed by Cardinal's words; Leclerc's intended role as representative *reader* ultimately empowers her as *writer* as well.

Moreover, and this is the second aspect of Cardinal's practice of the feminist essay that seems of particular interest here, the nature of the collaboration between Cardinal and Leclerc results in a dialogic text that is distinctively intersubjective, fluid, rhythmical, mutual, and multiple. Indeed, *In Other Words* and *Woman to Woman,* a similarly conceived and structured dialogue between Marguerite Duras and Xavière Gauthier, are the two key texts from which Suzanne Lamy (37–51) develops her theory of the specificity of female dialogue. Lamy's description of what she finds most appealing about these writers' richly harmonious voices clearly recalls Cardinal's commitment to a perpetual divagation between the vague and the rule bound: "I love the disparity [of these voices], made in the image of our world of debris and embellishment, their consent to fertile wandering [*la divagation*], their refusal of all arbitrary organization. Themes file past and intersect: creativity, feminism, social structure, politics, temporality, sexuality . . ." (Lamy, 49, my translation). More generally, the dialogic nature of *In Other Words* provides a model for a vision of female identity as fluid and continuous, characterized by the interpenetration of self and other, that Cardinal shares with a number of American as well as French feminist writers. Once again, like Woolf, DuPlessis, and Cixous, among others, Cardinal also transforms the first-person essay into a dialogue or a chorus of female voices. Consistent with her view of collaboration, Cardinal also conceives the individual female voice as inherently pluralistic: "When I write, I always begin with something that I know, that I have lived, then it transforms, opens up, rambles [*divague*]; the 'I' could become 'she,' but 'she' is more myself than 'I.' 'I' is a mask" (21).

And yet, despite the clear importance of *In Other Words* for an understanding of Marie Cardinal, despite the particular interest it will hold for readers of *The Words to Say It*, and even given the significance of the essay within a larger theoretical context, one might still have the right to wonder why American readers in general should welcome the translation in 1995 of a work originally published almost twenty years ago. The steady appearance over the last decade of English-language editions of a number of French feminist texts that date from the same period as *In Other Words* (1977) — for example, Hélène Cixous's and Catherine Clément's *The Newly Born Woman* (1975, 1986); Cixous's *"Coming to Writing" and Other Essays* (1976, 1991); Duras's and Gauthier's *Woman to Woman* (1974, 1987); and Claudine Herrmann's *The Tongue Snatchers* (1976, 1989) — at once confirms the significance of the work done by French feminists in the mid-1970s and offers clear evidence that the interest it stirred up even then among American feminists continues into the present.

Most anglophone readers were first introduced to French feminism in 1980 through the writers anthologized in *New French Feminisms*, edited by Elaine Marks and Isabelle de Courtivron. This widely known anthology included selections from a number of texts that would eventually be translated in their entirety; notably, Cixous's "The Newly Born Woman," Herrmann's "The Tongue Snatchers," and both Annie Leclerc's "Woman's Word" and "The Love Letter" initially appeared in excerpt here. In their editorial preface, Marks and Courtivron announce *New French Feminisms* as "the beginning of an exchange" (ix), one that will subsequently unfold within a comparative context that the structure of their own anthology did much to establish. Although Marks and Courtivron immediately acknowledge "certain surface resemblances" (ix) between French feminisms and American feminisms, they choose to focus on the "important differences": "We hope that by examining differences and specificity, by confronting modes of writing, thinking, and acting, we will be able to enlarge the scope of the discussion, to enrich our understanding of women and feminism, of words and acts" (x). The very success of this endeavor may well explain the initially puzzling absence of Cardinal from the pages of *New French Feminisms*.

As we now know, focused comparison between French and American feminisms—no doubt the kind of "confrontation" that the editors of *New French Feminisms* originally had in mind—quickly evolved into something more akin to cross-cultural conflict. Betsy Draine, in her 1989 review essay in *Signs*, "Refusing the Wisdom of Solomon: Some Recent Feminist Literary Theory," uses the biblical parable of Solomon to symbolize the current state of the enduring battle, "by now agonizingly familiar," that still opposes "two feminisms. . . . fighting to gain custody of feminist theory" (145): "The idea of the French/American split—once, perhaps, a useful heuristic—now presents itself as a reductively binary frame, encouraging intolerance and preventing fresh perceptions of feminist issues. The obvious challenge is to create a new context wide enough to comprehend the many kinds of feminist literary inquiry" (148). Similarly, in "Issues for an International Feminist Literary Criticism," a 1993 essay that constitutes *Signs'* most recent review of feminist literary scholarship, Amy Kaminsky continues to lament "the tenacity of the hold that the Franco-American dance has on feminist literary discussion" (213). In explicit agreement with Draine that "the differences between the two [feminisms] have devolved into a dichotomy that has often seemed to occupy the whole field of feminist literary criticism" (213), Kaminsky focuses on yet another consequence of this dangerous "schism" (214): the marginalization of feminist literary theory and criticism of all other national origins. "To date," she notes, "work on non-French-European, Latin American, Asian, African, and diasporan/postcolonial literature remains marginal" (218) as does "work written by women of color in the United States" (216). Kaminsky's subsequent discussion explores both works that extend our knowledge of international feminist scholarship "beyond the French" (216) and books whose "critical methodology would please Draine" inasmuch as they "happily and fruitfully synthesize French and Anglo-American approaches" (214). That Cardinal should now be included, albeit by name alone and only indirectly, through a passing reference to Françoise Lionnet's literary criticism (218), is entirely appropriate.

Ironically, in their search for feminist theory that "makes the link between the work on language that many French-trained feminists see as central to cultural transformation and the investigation of women's material conditions that has become identified with Anglo-American feminism" (Draine 154), both Draine and Kaminsky cite only the texts of American feminists. What Draine, like a great many other feminist scholars before her, identifies yet again as the crux of Franco-American theoretical disagreement—i.e., "the radical conflict between assumptions about language prevailing in French and American critical contexts" (164)—

passes in silence over another kind of linguistic problem that
has no doubt played an equally significant role in disrupting
efforts to establish cross-cultural communication. In the
United States, notes Kaminsky, feminist scholars continue to
be "handicapped by a lack of knowledge of foreign languages," making us "truly dependent on each other" for the
discovery of women writing in another language (222). In
that event, the publication of the English-language translation of Cardinal's *In Other Words* could not be more timely.

All of Marie Cardinal's work, but especially *In Other
Words*, given its explicitly theoretical and critical orientation,
offers a particularly useful response to Draine's call for the
creation of a new context within which to explore more
broadly and comprehensively contemporary feminist scholarship. Because Cardinal's writing consistently embodies the
interests of francophone and anglophone feminists, it also
points the way toward their theoretical and textual reconcili
ation. (In part, no doubt, this results from her multi-cultural
upbringing and background. Born and raised in Algeria,
Cardinal's adult life has been spent almost equally in France
and in Quebec. Consequently, her work has also been particularly important of late to feminist theorists such as
Françoise Lionnet and Winifred Woodhull in their explora-
tion of non-European literatures and postcolonial dis-
courses.) Indeed, Cardinal often expresses her concerns in
the very terms used by Draine and others. Thus the final
summary paragraphs of *In Other Words* call precisely for the
re(dis)covery of the link between language and women's
material condition (cf. Draine 154):

> It is this that we have forgotten: the soul of matter. . . .
> Women still perceive it, either consciously or unconsciously.
> But they don't know how or don't dare to say it, because the
> roads which lead from matter to words fall into the gutters of
> vocabulary, or they pass by so many barriers and filters that
> are so efficient that nothing remains of the living matter

when the words come from our mouths. Words are used
more and more often to hide sex and the body. (171)

Throughout *In Other Words,* Cardinal articulates and
illustrates an understanding of language and of women's
writing that has the potential to break down the linguistic and
discursive barriers that have hindered French and Anglo-
American cooperation in the field of feminist theory. As
Draine reminds us most recently, Anglo-American feminists
have repeatedly accused their French counterparts of some
or all of the following: "of creating a chimera in the notion of
a separate women's language"; "of elaborating the ideal of
women's writing in such a way as to align Women with the
body"; of "intellectual elitism (in their deployment of difficult
rhetorics and specialized vocabularies)"; "of excessive de-
pendence on male mentors"; of "citing male writers, almost
exclusively, as exemplars of feminine writing"; of failing to
analyze the material conditions that have kept women from
writing"; "of denying the material reality of women's oppression"; "of failing to oppose (vigorously enough) pornography,
rape, and other violence against women"; and finally, "of
deserting the field of political action for the field of contem-
plation/writing" (Draine 146–47).

For Cardinal, too, any notion of a separate women's
language is "a chimera": "I don't think that there is a masculine or feminine writing" (65). Indeed, she views such a belief
as not only false but unproductive and even potentially dangerous; it would allow men at present to deny all responsibility for the material conditions of women's oppression and,
even more importantly, eventually prevent them, and thus
humanity as a whole, from reaping the benefits that will
accrue in the future from a specifically feminist approach to
linguistic reform. For Cardinal does argue that speech and
writing are not only inseparable from the reality of women's
(and men's) lives but that discursive practices are therefore
also central to the development of strategies for political

change: "Speech is an act. Words are objects. . . . Men hermetically sealed these words, imprisoned women within them. Women must open them if they want to survive. It is an enormous, dangerous, and revolutionary task that we undertake" (41).

Given such a task, which requires that one write "brutally and disrespectfully," elitist discourse — "technical, scientific, or specialized language" (72) — constitutes a dangerous temptation for women. Cardinal joins Anglo-American feminists — and stands virtually alone among French feminists — by virture of her willingness to engage in an explicit critique of such theoreticians of *écriture féminine* as Hélène Cixous and Catherine Clément and their male mentors — notably, Roland Barthes, Gilles Deleuze, and Michel Foucault. Not only is their writing "incomprehensible for the majority of the public" (73), but its false neutrality serves to deny and/or to erase the bodies and the sexuality of its practitioners: "Technical words have no sex" (72). Thus Cardinal also rejects the temptation to "feminize language": "It seems to me that this would be to create a new alienation by creating a new specialized language" (77).

Yet Cardinal's conviction that "speech is an act" and "words are objects" clearly equates linguistic expression with social change and experiential existence. The sense of lexical constraint that Cardinal experiences as a woman writer — "cither because I don't have the words or because the French words are so invested with meaning by men that they betray me when I, a woman, use them" (77) — focuses, in particular, on women's relationship to their bodies. In this domain, Cardinal believes that language has the power to generate new words that will in turn produce a new reality:

> Gap. Opening. Night. False night. . . . What word will make my cunt exist? What word would express its inertness, simultaneously active and somber. A hole. A well. A steamer.

A sleeve. . . . To explain the sweetness of its dampness, the
depth of its abyss? Footpath. Gully. Vagina. Stem. To explain
the carmine road of sexual pleasure, for the child. And the
commonplace story of the blood? The bloody sex? (78)

If, on the one hand, Cardinal shows us in such passages what
it might actually mean for a woman to "write the body" into
existence, on the other hand, her linguistic experimentation
and her expression of the body are always directly connected
to the social, political, and material conditions of women's
lives.

As a result, Cardinal often uses the subject of physical
violence to discuss the specificity of women's bodies and
language. Near the center of *In Other Words,* rape suddenly
appears as a brutal rupture in the text that will delay its
publication for months. Even though Cardinal escapes rape
by pretending to suffer a heart attack, the curious idea that
occurs to her in the very midst of her simulation—"I thought
of my glasses, 'If he takes them I won't be able to write'"
(105)—clearly establishes the connection between the threat
of rape and women's creative possibilities, and Cardinal's
subsequent terror indeed leaves her temporarily unable to
work. As Cardinal's reflections on the vulnerability of the
female body evolve into social critique and revolt, she specifically calls for an end to women's learned passivity and collaboration in their own submission. In this context, the connection between language and sexuality announces a
defensive—and offensive—strategy that responds precisely
to her express desire to find the word that will "make [her]
cunt exist."

Cardinal's key word *open*—"Women must open
[words] if they want to survive" (41)—thus fuses in its double
meaning female language and female sexuality; open language—accessible to all: unhampered by restrictions, free of
prejudice, receptive to new ideas—corresponds to the open
body—accessible to all: exposed, without protection, afford-

ing unobstructed passage. But their superimposition produces a paradoxical inversion, for a writing freed to explore
the female body ultimately serves to restore and preserve its
integrity:

> The best way to prove that words are lacking, that French
> isn't made for women, is to put ourselves in close proximity
> with our bodies, to express the unexpressed and to use the
> French vocabulary as it is, directly, without cleaning it up.
> It will thus become evident and clear that there are things
> that we can't translate into words. How do we describe our
> sex, gestation as it is lived, time, the duration of women? We
> must invent. The language will become more feminine, it
> will open up, be embellished and enriched. Our sisterhood
> will be fertile and welcoming because our words will be
> useful to everyone. (71)

Even as Cardinal encourages women to produce texts that
would "write the body" primarily, she does so in a context in
which she explicitly—and repeatedly—rejects the notion of
an *écriture féminine*, a specifically female language and discourse. The linguistic feminizing required for the adequate
expression of female reality enriches language as a whole.

For the moment, however, Cardinal does acknowledge that distinctions continue to be made between the work
of female and male writers at the point of its reception: "I
don't think that there is a masculine or feminine writing. But
I do believe that there is a difference in reading according to
whether the words were written by a man or a woman" (65–
66). Cardinal's call for linguistic "openness" clearly also em-
braces the critical concern she repeatedly expresses with
issues of literacy and accessibility: "An unreadable book is a
censored book" (74). Her own texts, and especially *The Words
to Say It* and *In Other Words,* are, in keeping with the imagery
of their titles, empowering in their readability. They open up
a variety of paths on which different readers may wander,
often toward writing of their own. Thus the "musings on

Marie Cardinal's text," which serve Toni Morrison to introduce and clarify the subject matter of an essay devoted to
American literature (x), offer only the most recent example of
how the richly productive context of Cardinal's work can
incite her readers to speak and to write "in other words" in
their own turn.

WORKS CITED

Abel, Elizabeth. "Editor's Introduction." *Critical Inquiry* 8 (1981):
173–78.
Bosselet, Dominique. "Maintenant, Marie Cardinal reçoit des lettres
d'hommes." *Le Matin de Paris,* 24 February 1972: 27.
Cardinal, Marie. *Devotion and Disorder* (1987). Trans. Karin Montin.
London: The Women's Press, 1991.
———. *The Words to Say It* (1975). Trans. Patricia Goodheart.
Preface and Afterword by Bruno Bettelheim. Cambridge: Van
Vactor and Goodheart, 1983.
Cixous, Hélène. *"Coming to Writing" and Other Essays.* Trans. Sarah
Cornell, Deborah Jenson, Ann Liddle, Susan Sellers. Cambridge:
Harvard University Press, 1991.
———. "The Laugh of the Medusa" (1975). Trans. Paula Cohen and
Keith Cohen. *Signs* 1 (1976): 875–93.
Cixous, Hélène, and Catherine Clément. *The Newly Born Woman*
(1975). Trans. Betsy Wing. Minneapolis: University of Minnesota
Press, 1991.
Draine, Betsy. "Refusing the Wisdom of Solomon: Some Recent
Feminist Literary Theory." *Signs* 15 (1989): 144–70.
DuPlessis, Rachel Blau. "For the Etruscans." *The New Feminist
Criticism,* ed. Elaine Showalter. New York: Pantheon Books, 1985.
Duras, Marguerite, and Xavière Gauthier. *Woman to Woman* (1974).
Trans. Katharine A. Jensen. Lincoln: University of Nebraska
Press, 1987.
Gallop, Jane. "Annie Leclerc Writing a Letter with Vermeer." *The
Poetics of Gender,* ed. Nancy K. Miller. New York: Columbia
University Press, 1986.
Herrmann, Claudine. *The Tongue Snatchers* (1976). Trans. Nancy
Kline. Lincoln: University of Nebraska Press, 1989.
Kaminsky, Amy. "Issues for an International Feminist Literary Criti-
cism." *Signs* 19 (1993): 213–27.

Lamy, Suzanne. *d'elles*. Montreal: Hexagone, 1979.

Lionnet, Françoise. *Autobiographical Voices: Race, Gender, and Self-Portraiture*. Ithaca: Cornell University Press, 1989.

Marks, Elaine, and Isabelle de Courtivron, eds. *New French Feminisms*. Amherst: University of Massachusetts Press, 1980.

Morrison, Toni. *Playing in the Dark: Whiteness and the Literary Imagination*. New York: Vintage Books, 1992.

Woolf, Virginia. *A Room of One's Own* (1929). New York: Harcourt, 1957.

Woodhull, Winifred. *Transfigurations of the Maghreb: Feminism, Decolonization, and Literatures*. Minneapolis: University of Minnesota Press, 1993.

The importance and scope of Marie Cardinal's work has not come fully to the attention of women today. Yet Cardinal's experience is the experience of many women, and she writes this experience in the words of many women. *In Other Words* is a work in which Cardinal's primary concerns are words and voice. Because of this, Cardinal's translator is challenged to keep both words and voice true to the original.

It has been my aim to remain true to Cardinal's voice, be that the speaking voice that she uses in her discussions with Annie Leclerc, or the prose voice she uses in her descriptive passages, at once poetic and powerfully truthful. As Cardinal moves from subject to subject and thought to thought, she works each into the past, the present, and the future of her life as well as into the lives of women in general. Cardinal doesn't shy away from any topic, and she uses words that specifically, almost brutally, address her subjects. The words are her arms, her means of fighting the stereotypes and prejudices that all women face. Her own words and voice remain strong in the face of lovers, husbands, mothers, friends. Cardinal places emphasis on both the sound and use of language. She writes of words as they are and words as she would like them to be. Her words are opened up or closed; they are living, breathing entities. Words are the means of war, life, love, existence.

To be true to these words has meant that some of my diction may be awkward to the ear of readers looking for the voice of an American English speaker. American English is very different from French in many ways: it is not as willing to tolerate long and complex sentences. Nor is it willing to accept incomplete sentences and fragments as entire thoughts. It is not as able to describe the relationships between words in a sentence. Often, it is not as flexible, not as expansive, not as evocative. There are, therefore, a very few words or phrases that I have left in the original French. Some of these derive from the absolute lack of an English equivalent (*Pieds-Noir*, for example). Other expressions are left simply in order to remain true to the sense and texture of Cardinal's language (for example, the French folk song quoted in the text). There are also instances where, to remain true to the voice of the author, I have used long or incomplete sentences. Robert Classo, an Italian publisher, has said: "The mark of a good translation is not its fluency, but rather all those unusual and original formulations ('Not the way to say it') that the translator has been bold enough to preserve and defend." I hope that, in bringing this text into English, I have preserved and defended enough of these original formulations to convey the uniqueness, passion, and power of Marie Cardinal's writing.

For her permission to embark on this translation and for her continued interest in its progress and publication, I would like to thank Marie Cardinal. For their help and support at the many different stages of this project, I would like to thank Joan Catapano, Mary Beth Haas, Kathryn Stafford, Serafina Clarke, and Marilyn Gaddis Rose. For his continued support, I thank Jim Bork.

Amy Cooper

In Other Words

Preface

I meet many people, as it happens (twenty-six meetings, debates, conferences, etc., in the past five months) and I
receive thousands of letters. In my replies, whether verbal or
written, I maintain a laconic attitude which does not profoundly engage me, an attitude that is, in some respect, only an
acknowledgment. I don't want to establish genuine ties with
those who approach me; I haven't the time, the means, or the
right. I am a woman in the process of living; besides, I am no
longer the one who wrote the books that gave rise to this
audience and this mail. I can't answer the questions others ask

me, and I can't give the advice they ask of me, because I ask
these questions of myself and I, too, request this advice.

To tell the truth, I still feel an inadequacy, a bewilder-
ment, a yearning in my soul: these people tell me their names,
their anxieties or their joys, they tell me their age, their work,
very often they make an enormous effort to express themselves; and I, in exchange, send them a "Thank you, thank
you, I'm very touched. . . . Sincerely yours, etc.," for fear of
giving them too much of my time, of revealing my own
ignorance, of claiming an importance for each one that I don't
have, and that I don't want to have. Yet it is true that I'm
touched, that I want to talk with them, want to exchange
words, want to say, don't really want to write.

The following pages are, therefore, often spoken
pages. I want to emphasize this fact if only because these
days, more and more often, we hand over printed conversations to the public without warning them of it, conversations
about personalities, champions, stars, and we make readers
believe that this is literature. In exchange for a few million,
we make X, Y, or Z speak into a tape recorder and then we ask
a ghost writer, for a few dollars, to make this into a "clean
copy": black on white . . . and we bring the book by X, Y, or Z
to bookstores on a silver platter. It's a hoax that does an
enormous wrong to those who write, a commercial process
that creates fewer and fewer writers, researchers, published
poets. Because to write is another thing altogether!

Still, the spoken word has qualities which writing
doesn't have. Speech is fluidity, transition, current. Spoken
words do not have the density of written words. You must
always keep that in mind as you read the words that follow.
Spoken words have no exemplary value, no stability. It is in
this way that they coincide with my desire to communicate
and with my reflection, which is only a pause, a temporary
halt on the road to understanding, which is interminable,
since it extends constantly.

But I do not deceive myself by the fact that these words are printed and that they therefore mimic writing. To speak, then to transcribe this speech onto paper with printed characters, and finally to publish this transcription, all of this constitutes a series of actions which, because of its conclusion (publication), is suspect. I'm aware of this. In all honesty, I must once again warn the reader that this book isn't really a book; it is a reflection spoken aloud, a conversation with others.

I don't deceive myself there either, for "others," under the circumstances, is Annie Leclerc, because it is with her that I spoke. Besides, it is difficult to identify Annie with the anonymity of "others." Annie is a woman who has written wonderful books, who is well informed, intelligent, young, and pretty. I respect Annie a great deal. I like her strictness, her severity, her desire for the truth, her incandescence, and her physical fragility. But I also like the fact that she wanders, that she searches like me, like all of those whom I've met or who have written to me. As they have, she too has constructed an idea about me through my books, and she asks me questions, on the one hand to force me to explain myself more clearly, to show the woman that I am rather than the writer; and on the other hand, she asks because she believes that my answers will be able to help her to progress as well. She reveals herself in this way, the direction of her curiosity, and her interest.

This, then, is what these pages are: a walk through the consciousness of two people, a desire to meet each other, a common will to be honest, whether in laughter, in indecency, or in the solemnity of words that we put forward without knowing exactly what they contain.

Annie Leclerc lives in a lane in the 13th arrondissement of Paris. It is a lane with pock-marked paving, with houses intimately squeezed together on one side. On the other side, there are naked walls which are high in places. In a hollow, these walls give way to I'm not sure what kind of architectural attempt, a low, modern building which makes you ask yourself what it is doing there. In this gently climbing lane there are a few trees whose branches move above the walls, a bit of grass, and a great variety of dog turds. Annie's house is narrow. The window on the ground floor looks onto the street. Because I came early in the morning, I often saw this window opened into a well-lived-in room; I never could tell whether it was a bedroom or a parlor. In reality, Annie's house is double, the front building hides another just like it. Between the two there is a courtyard on the ground floor and a narrow passageway on the second.

If I tell you all of this, it isn't to intrude upon Annie's privacy but to say that this general effect is extremely Mediterranean. You might believe that you're in a house in Algiers' Casbah. A fig tree could grow in the courtyard, pots of verbena could be in the windows, the washing could be drying on the terraces. And perhaps there really is a fig tree, verbena or terraces. . . . Annie's husband is Greek.

The room where we spoke is upstairs, it is small, it is Annie's office. A table, a chair, books, a typewriter, papers, an old sofa that I claimed on the first day and never surrendered thereafter, a French window opening onto the narrow passageway which spans the courtyard, where ivy and mint grow. And a red telephone, of unusual Parisian design, the most beautiful telephone I've ever seen.

The telephone excepted, this decor could have been that of my childhood.

But also, because of the lane, the sofa, and the speech—because of the speech especially—these moments could have been psychoanalysis sessions.

In this way, the two most important elements of my life, the Mediterranean and psychoanalysis, were reunited there, in that place which was otherwise totally foreign to me.

Psychoanalysis will often be the subject of these pages. This is normal; an analysis never ends. It is a way of thinking, a way of living life. Once the specifically medical period is over, when the sick person no longer is sick, when she feels responsible and capable of existing without her doctor, analysis continues. As a result, I will speak of it; I cannot do otherwise. Yet I won't speak like the "specialists." I don't like the way they manipulate psychoanalysis, putting it into any sort of work, using its vocabulary for everything and nothing. I, who was a patient, who was saved by my analysis, who followed the road with a doctor for seven years before being able to walk alone, I understand nothing of what these psychoanalytic specialists say.

Often I have heard "feminist analysts" attack Freud and bombard me with quotes from the work of this "great misogynist," each one more difficult than the other for women to tolerate. It is only one step from this to the deduction that psychoanalysis is not made for women. But I've discovered that I am a woman, what it means "to be a woman," thanks to the most Freudian type of analysis there is. . . .

I believe that there is a great difference between those who have been cured by psychoanalysis of a neurosis which kept them from living and those who know all about psycho-analytic theory, including didactic analysis. Curiously, the lives and purposes of the first group gradually become more clear, while the lives and purposes of the second group gradually become more obscure. And yet, it is with the aid of the second group that the first has been cured. . . . It seems to me that analytic theory, at least that which concerns mental illness, cannot be popularized. As for its applications, peda-gogical, sociological, etc., perhaps a new vocabulary must be created, different from that of therapy. I have often heard extremely disturbed neurotics, currently in analysis, whose only companion in their alienation is suicide, become infatu-ated with the fact that "their transfer wasn't taking place in the right phase of their cure," or that their "regression wasn't in agreement with their Oedipus complex because of the sadistic-anal frustration caused by their analyst. . . ." How were they ever going to escape! I was terrified. While listen-ing to them I never stopped thinking of what my analyst said to me the first day: "Don't use any of the notions that you have, find a vocabulary that comes naturally to you."

At Annie's house, because her house was familiar to me from the outset—more than because of Annie herself, whom I feared a bit—it was easy for me to use a vocabulary natural to me, my everyday words.

First, Annie wanted me to speak of my family, of Algeria. That didn't mean much to me: these subjects belonged to the world that I wanted to write about and that, moreover, I never stop writing about. But I thought that it wasn't necessary to begin with concealment, that a bridge between her and me had to be established. Since that was what she offered me, and since I had nothing else to offer her, I had to make use of it. So I began to speak of Algeria and of my family.

I hadn't taken the unconscious into account, which is the best guardian of my frailties. But he is a blind guardian, a despot, who does his job with such enthusiasm that he keeps locked away in oblivion the keys which my conscious needs to progress. To coax him, I must parley, travel all the well-marked paths which lead toward him, and demonstrate that I am safe. Then, if he is convinced, he opens a door and lets the living, pulsing memory pass.

At Annie's house, because I was intimidated on the first day, perhaps also because I didn't want to talk about that, the unconscious double-locked the doors. I spoke, nevertheless; I spoke without stopping. But what did I say? I will never know because I remember that at the end I pushed the wrong button on the tape recorder.

Annie said: "It can't be, it can't be! We lost all of it?"

"Yes."

"But you have to tell all of that."

"Well, then, I'll write it afterward, when I write the book."

Here we are:

I left Algeria exactly twenty years ago, just after the birth of my second child, my daughter Alice. She was one month old and my son was two when I left. On that day, I didn't know that I would never return. If I had known it, I would have scrutinized the details of details, I would have had the time, the heat, the light, the faces imprinted in me. As it is, I no longer even remember if I took the plane or the boat. I have only the memories of a young woman who travels with young children, one in her arms, the other clinging to her skirt. Problems with baggage, bottles, beds. . . . It was summer, it must have been very hot, it must have smelled like urine, dust and sweat, the sky must have been white. I didn't even watch my land disappear behind me for the last time. The end of French Algeria was near but I didn't want to see it; there were still soldiers everywhere, weapons, identity checks. I was glad to take my children away from there, to go to France, to join my husband who had just received his degree. I only thought of that: of our newly born daughter whom he did not yet know, and of his new diploma.

We had spent a studious winter in Greece, at Salonika, where both of us were professors (I had taken the position left vacant by Michel Butor at the Lycée Français, and Jean-Pierre was a reader at the university).

The winter is cold in Salonika because of the Vardar wind. Each time it blows, you could say it pushes the Balkans in front of it. We lived in the neighborhood of Kalamari, the old Jewish neighborhood, where during the war the Germans had exterminated most of the citizens. The slaughter of these old Israelite families, in refuge there since the pogroms of Isabelle the Catholic, had been planned. Of this past-present there remained huge houses and villas surrounded by vacant and overgrown lots which had been parks. The rose bushes had returned to their wild state, reeds mixed with hibiscus, ancient gravel walkways were dissolving in weeds. Completely empty. Numerous poor families had invaded these devastated homes and the neighborhood had become populous, talkative, sincere. The nuns' convent chimed the hours.

Since I was teaching night courses for adults, I often came home late. In our house, an old woman with a heart condition lived on the ground floor. She would hear me open the door and call to me. She lived in warm obscurity where small, perpetual lamps flickered in front of her icons. She was sunk into a bed which rather resembled a trunk, she was white, gentle and maternal. She wanted to see my stomach and she felt it with satisfaction; the baby that would be born made her happy. Sometimes I sat down next to her for a moment. We spoke of the weather, the glazed streets, the neighborhood gossip that she had heard at the baker's, where all the women went to get the dinners which they had put into this good man's oven to simmer. He would open an infernal little door and, with a long shovel, adroitly search for the eggplant au gratin, the roasted goat, the stuffed tomatoes. The room where the women were seated next to each other on two benches smelled like herbs and spices and rustled with Greek voices relating the daily news. Thus, my neighbor kept me informed of all that happened in Kalamari. She gave me advice and made recommendations for the baby and then I went upstairs to my place.

Jean-Pierre had prepared dinner, had lit the stove in our room and had already begun to work. I stretched out on the bed and fell asleep. I liked the soft and muffled noise made by the pages of the large Greek and Latin dictionaries he often examined.

I thought of that in leaving my country, and of getting out of the crowd, of nothing other than that.

Today, I often dream of returning to Algiers, and I imagine that it will be as it was when I was little. It is no use to tell myself that nothing is the same, that my house is no longer in the village—that doesn't change the procession of images that my soul projects.

It is the end of the night, not entirely dawn. I am so excited at the idea of returning home that I haven't slept. I saw the obscurity clearing a bit in the rounded porthole. I can't stand it any longer. I get up, dress in the dark and creep onto the deck. It smells strongly of the sea, the boat, and caulked wood. There are the showy lights of other gangways and the blackness of the beach further in the distance. By watching, and perhaps also because I occasionally become drowsy, the time passes quickly. I see the horizon thicker in one place; it is land, it is my land. When I was little, each time I returned to Algiers I cried with happiness. (Perhaps I would cry today too if I returned.) I hated France, my well-mannered family, the kings and the castles, the victories, glories and monuments, the department stores, the boulevards, the moderate climate, the fine elegant rain of summer. For me, this was hell: always to be careful to hold yourself properly, eat properly, be dressed properly. Shit!

The sun burst out suddenly, as it always does there, already dazzling, already hot. I saw the coast clearly. I knew each of its beaches, each cove, each crag.

I often think of this return to my soil. I have a strong desire to be there again, to smell it, to take it in, to touch it. But at the same time I am afraid that if I return, I will be attacked and bound by the sticky jellyfish of sentiment, of tenderness, of family memories. I already think of Saint-Eugène cemetery where my father and sister are buried; I am afraid to go there, to take refuge on the white slab where their names are engraved, similar to my own, and no longer to move from it, considering it my home from that moment on. Yet I know very little—or nothing at all—of these two dead people who lie there like mocking sentinels of a past, detestable history. I'm afraid of ghosts dressed up in colonial helmets or with lace parasols. I'm afraid of large airy houses whose doors will be closed to me. I'm afraid of the ruins of war. I'm afraid of the voices which will call out to me from everywhere, the streets, the gardens, my school, the estates, the harbor, the hills, the country. I believe that I would hear them, that I would even instigate their cries, their laughter or their groans; perhaps I would let myself be taken by them. Yet I am only attracted by the earth itself, the earth as it is: difficult to cultivate, red, dry, favorable for thyme and mastic trees, sea pine and vineyards, hot. Too hot.

In the end, what I fear is to be confronted with the truth of my love for this land that I owned. I was born there as a landowner, the daughter of a landowner, granddaughter of a landowner, great-granddaughter, . . . etc. Would I just be able to pass through it? Would I be able to look at it as I look at the rest of the world? And what if I wasn't capable of feeling the pure love, without greediness or spite, that I think I hold for this land? I am so persuaded that the fact of possession is a cancer, that I ask myself if I will not discover a filthy wound there, in the beloved land where my roots are sunk. And that I would find this even if I didn't want possession of this land, even if I had wished for the exact opposite.

I belonged to a family of colonists who are proud of their colonization, proud of the hardships they had suffered to cultivate the soil. Furthermore, there was something to be proud of when you saw vineyards groove the countryside all the way to the horizon, when you walked in overpoweringly fragrant orange groves where checkerboards of sun and shadow embroidered the plains.

One hundred years, it took them scarcely one hundred years to see an Algeria that had been stripped by conquest covered with vineyards, grain and citrus fruits. In my family we spoke often of the salty earth that had to be made pure; of the swamps, infested with malaria-carrying mosquitoes, which had to be drained; of this country twice conquered: by soldiers and by laborers. The colonists had in-

vested so much in this harsh soil, where the first children
were born and where the first dead were buried; they had
given so much to this remote and savage land that they didn't
consider their farms to be acquisitions or appropriations but
private property, fruit of their sweat, their courage, and their
tenacity. Even more so because at the beginning, they alone
made Algeria. For, in 1830, in this country which was almost
five times larger than France, there were only, in terms of
manpower, a few nomadic tribes dispersed throughout the
territory, less than a million inhabitants. It is later that the
Arabs multiplied and were made to sweat, erasing the difference, as it were, between the Arabs themselves and the goats
that they kept.

I belonged to one of those families who, from generation to generation, said: "You see the road lined with eucalyptus that goes from Aboukir to Mostaganem?" "The big road?"
"Yes; well, it was your great-great-grandfather who laid it out
and planted the trees in 1847." I saw the immense eucalyptus
trees with their small blue leaves and their trunks scaled by
long blazes of red. For me, these magnificent trees were my
first great-grandfather. He watched my comings and goings
between school and the farm. He stayed awake during my
star-filled nights, where jackals howled. "You know the valley
that goes from there to there?" "Yes." "Well, it was your great-
grandfather who brought over the new refugees from France
during the war of 1870 and settled them there. He baptized
the villages. Only reeds grew there before." These villages,
where pomegranate trees and roses flowered, were called the
"valley of the gardens," "the hamlet beneath the forest. . . ."
They were refreshing in the hottest part of the summer, but
that didn't make the soil any better. It had to be worked again
and again to become as green as it is now.

The History of France, the History of Algeria, and the
History of my family was all one; for me it was the History of the
world. It began in 1837 with the arrival of our first ancestor on

the soil of Oran: a young aristocrat from Bordeaux, a marquis (it appears that this title is rarely legitimate . . .), who owned land and castles. On his arm, a young woman with whom he seemed hopelessly in love (according to the hallowed expression). She was the wife of a notary. The love that they felt for each other was so strong that they decided to flee (at that time divorce was inconceivable) and to hide their passion far from everyone. Algeria had just been conquered.

This ancestor brought goods, belongings, money. What is more, as soon as he arrived, they granted him an allotment of a few thousand hectares to clear and till. If he drew something from the land, it would belong to him in twenty years.

The lover/great-grandfather began by hiring manpower: Spaniards, Frenchmen, Italians, adventurers from Mediterranean ports; then he had a large farm built, just like those of his country. It was a fortified farm, however: the buildings and gardens were guarded by high walls of which only a few sections remained one hundred years later, those on which the enormous front gate leaned.

He knew vineyards, this great-grandfather. They had already made his fortune in France. It didn't take him long to cover the countryside with them, in spite of the sand and the heat. He grew vines which gave a strongly alcoholic wine, exactly the wine that was missing in Bordeaux, to rejuvenate the thin wine of rainy seasons. . . .

When he died, there were vineyards and olive trees surrounding the house everywhere, as far as the eye could see, every way you turned. This was the earth which supported my family until 1962.

I know this earth by heart. I know all of it. I know where its grapes are the best, the sweetest, I know where the fattest olives grow. I know the smallest of its vales, I know where erosion has laid its stones bare like bones, I know how the rain turns it red. I know where it grows wild tulips, broom, and

daisies. I know the hiding places of porcupines, of its chame-
leons and turtles, the dens of its jackals. I know each of its Arab
shacks, each of its retaining walls, and its tent villages; I know
the roads and even the short cuts that lead to these places, the
odor of burnt vines which announces them. I know the melody
of the flute at dusk, which heralds the calm of its nights.

Above all, I know what it taught me: not only the
progress of its ants, the madness of its wind, but also the
mystery of its gestations. I know the teeming velocity of
decomposition in the unchangeable weight of the heat, the
happiness of drinking when you are thirsty, the misfortune of
not drinking when you are thirsty. My body has been wrought
by it. It will always know how to grapple with the world only
as the land has taught me to grapple with it. The soles of my
feet know the smoothness of its mud and the roughness of its
rock. My throat has been formed by its music and by its
language. I have no other rhythms but these.

What is troubling is that my mother the puritan, my
grandmother the worldly woman, my great-grandmother the
saint . . . each had the same love that I have for this land. In
our family's jargon, we call it "the hamlet," "the big farm,"
"the little farm," or simply "the farm." What tied us to the
hamlet, like that which tied the Pieds-Noir to Algeria, was a
passionate love in which material interest didn't play a great
part. Far from it. It was made up of an attachment from the
core of themselves, the bond which ties those who suffer to
the cause of the pain, with an unreasonable passion and love
at first sight: we were in love with Algeria.

The country was large, the farms immense. Each
family lived on its land as if in a kingdom. The colonist was at
once father, lord, and proprietor, he exercised his rights and
duties as if in the Middle Ages or the nineteenth century.
People lived under a regime of bourgeois feudality that we
will call paternalism, this cancer of the stomach.

Until they found oil, Algeria held no interest for

France, which took its cannon fodder from it, dispatched its adventurers and its legionnaires there, sold its manufactured goods there, bought its wine. For the most part, France let its poorly raised children do as they pleased and thanked God that they were far away; before the Algerian war, I never heard that the sweat of the Arabs disturbed our motherland's sense of smell, whether that odor spread through the vineyards or through the battle field.

The man whom we called a "francaoui," the Frenchman from France, was a pretentious gentleman, speaking sharply, hawking culture and traditions. Often, he was a man puny in stature, but he had manners and, as he appreciated pretty women and money, it wasn't rare that he returned to his mother country with both, either to regild his family coat of arms or to revive his blood. He made us feel that, in the hierarchy of civilization, we were precisely one step below him, and we didn't contest it because all that came from France was the best there was. To marry a "francaoui" was a promotion. When it came to French Algeria, France maintained this colonialist behavior which we will also call paternalism, this cancer of the mind.

Cancer of the stomach and mind, generalized cancer, then. Generalized stupidity, complicated by a total absence of politicizing, which at the last moment would bring about the OAS. French Algeria could only die. It died in terrible spasms, unforgettable for those who lived through them. France, in her entirety, was marked by the agony of French Algeria. For the "little Frenchmen" of the contingent saw horrors there that they should never have seen, and a million repatriated people corrupted the continent with their infectious wounds. The French Algerians form an illegitimate people which is neither French nor Algerian, whose history isn't long enough to form a nation, but is sufficiently long to make their last generation unassimilable. Away from their homes, they are like worms crawling in fruit. The Atridae cannot be imported.

So, from my mother, who participates more than anyone else in my upbringing—not only because she is my mother, but also because she was terrible, Clytemnestra, Electra, and Iphigenia by turns—from her I have no mother-land (because I no longer have the right to call Algeria so), and no name, for the son of this first romantic ancestor took his mother's married name, that is the name of the cuckolded notary from Bordeaux. . . .

By my father I have a name: Cardinal, and a national-ity: French. My father was an engineer, poisoned by gas during World War I and sent by the army, in 1918, to construct hangars for dirigibles in Algeria, in Baraki. He stayed there, married my mother, who was much younger than he and whom he divorced the very year of my birth. My mother detested him. Even more: she abhorred him. He died in 1946. I was an adolescent, almost a child. I didn't know him; I knew nothing of him.

During the course of our conversations, Annie often made me realize that all within me is a mix of uncertainty and rules. I never knew exactly if she wanted me, personally, to define myself in those terms, or if she wanted to come to a general conclusion from this: women are both vague and rule bound. I feel that at the time she was groping about the boundaries of the vague and the rule bound and that I was a good guinea pig for her because it is true that I need rules. It is from these rules that I can wander, and I don't know how to live if I don't wander.

In *Perlimplin's Love*, Federico García Lorca evokes an "unrooted and floating jasmine." I have always identified myself with this jasmine. This is a laughable pretension if you think that jasmine is a climbing plant, light, slender, unas-suming, with tapering leaves and star-shaped flowers of white or pearl color, while I am a caryatid, a tall athletic woman, weighty, present, clumsy.

It is true that the rule is that jasmine is "a shrub

belonging to the Oleaceae family," and that as such, it lives in a specific manner, requires a certain soil, a certain climate, and a certain humidity to grow. But jasmine is above all a heavy perfume which insinuates itself everywhere, which wars with the smells of men and the smells of work. When it is in full bloom and the wind blows from the Atlas, it isn't unusual for jasmine to perfume the streets of Algiers. It comes from the country in breaths, descends the sloping alleyways, mingles with the trams and the autos. You smell it, you say to yourself, "It is the end of spring," "the wind is coming from the mountains," "the fishermen will have trouble getting back to port," "soon we'll have grapes," "soon there will be no more water." When you no longer smell it, when it has disappeared from the street corners, life is without season, without reason, except the modern reasons to live. You smell it again, there is desire in its fragrance, you say to yourself "I'm going to make love tonight," "my stomach needs to be filled," "my daughter is going to be twenty," "my father has been dead how many years now?" Where is this jasmine? In what garden? Does it climb a palm tree, or the walls of a mosque, or is it behind the old fashioned iron gates of a colonial home?

Dark green shutters and blinds. Houses the color of sand, or a yellowed white, nearly ochre, dusty. Gardens of my memory. Palm trees. The rigid arcs of palm leaves tangle like poorly braided hair. The gray pigeon rises, snapping the already hot air of the morning with its flight. Geraniums. Nasturtiums. Yellow roses. Battered earth. The formal palm trees with their elephant skins are the phantoms of women in long dresses of white pique, men in Panama hats, little girls in hoop skirts, little boys in sailor suits. How far away and vague it is! How it is present, reborn each moment, obliterates itself, reappears. How many millions of threads compose the fabric of my life? How many lives do I have? Fortunately, I will never know!

Annie Leclerc: I want to know how it was before and why this snapped so that analysis became necessary.

Marie Cardinal: You are curious about that, but I am not. You see, I've found the roots that push into my "before." I know them well now and I know that the person that I was is indescribable. To tell about her, I would have to retell the history of Christianity, matriarchy, the colonization, money, etc. If I do not, I'm going to tell you entirely personal anecdotes and we'll arrive at the conclusion: it is because my father was like this and my mother was like that that I was something else. Which isn't satisfactory. It's true that because they were what they were, I am what I am. But what were they bearers of? It's what they conveyed that is interesting. If I want to speak of my "before," I'm obligated to go into all of that. You understand?

Annie: Certainly, each life is united with totality and you no longer know from which end to follow it.

Nevertheless, let's come back to you; there are three sequences in your life which seem to me very important: first, the time of your response to social and familial demands. Next, the time of the collapse, which was simultaneously a time of preparation for your birth. And finally, the time of true writing, which fundamentally occupies you.

These three periods are marked by extraordinarily clear symptoms. Well, there I'm bullying you a bit, I'm interfering in your life, I'm antagonizing you.

Marie: You know, you can't bully someone who has been through analysis. Unless of course they want to be bullied.

Annie: Because they already know much more about that?

Marie: They don't know more about it, but they have a taste for research, for quest, for enrichment; and they never refuse what comes to them because it always has to be analyzed, and consequently it is always interesting.

Annie: What struck me at first in *Les mots pour le dire* was the blood. Blood, blood, blood. . . . I was justified in being taken by this because it was this that seized you yourself. You evoke your childhood, your life as a woman, your life after analysis, and I learn a lot about blood, a blood that is the blood of a woman.

I learn that your first regular period was late, not until twenty. Then you became—as you yourself say—a "regulated" woman, with a husband, children. This is the time of the "before." You tell me, moreover, that you have never been a woman with a regular cycle, as it should be according to its terminology.

Marie: I have only been on a regular cycle with the pill.

Annie: Then you tell me that now, since you have moved into the realm of writing, of expression, you no longer have periods. As if you no longer needed them.

Marie: Yes, that's true. But before talking about that, I have to tell you the story of what happened to me Saturday.

Saturday I was invited by the library of a small village near Paris to come and talk about my book. While I was there, I saw a couple enter; the man was quite handsome and the woman was physically nondescript. Young people, in their mid- to late thirties, who didn't say a word the whole time. But when I neared the end, the man verbally attacked me. He asked me dryly why I spoke to people like that.

Annie: Not why you wrote like that?

Marie: No, why I had written the book and why I was now talking about it publicly. I told him that, personally, I had no desire whatsoever to talk about psychoanalysis, that I hadn't written a book about psychoanalysis. I had written the story of a woman in which psychoanalysis has great importance, even a primary importance. To me, this is my book, it is a moment in the life of a woman, a novel. Agreed, I lived all that the woman in the book lived, but I lived it from day to day. If I had made daily notes then and had published these notes once the analysis was finished, that would have been a document on psychoanalysis. But that isn't the case. Long after the end of my analysis, I decided to write about it, to make it into my sixth book, because in the meantime I had become a writer (which already makes me different from the woman in the book); and it is in the persona of the writer that I saw this story, not in the persona of the witness. So, there are parts of my analysis which have disappeared and others which are expanded. For example, I didn't write one word about the thrashings my mother gave me for no reason at all.

Yet they were often brought up during analysis because, still today, I am afraid of blows, afraid that someone will hurt me, without realizing that the spectacle of my mother's violence inhibited my own. So it was important, but as a writer, it bored me to write about it: either it was written in a realistic fashion and became a special case; or I transposed it into lyricism or into poetry, and this wasn't the tone of that book, a tone which had taken me years to find and which had possessed me from the very first page to the very last. On the other hand, my mother's confession of her unsuccessful attempt to abort me didn't have a great importance in my psychoanalysis because I had a very clear memory of this confession and I had drawn all possible conclusions about it before beginning treatment; so I didn't have to pry into that as much with the doctor. But in writing about it, it became enormous, it occupied a formidable place. I realized in writing it that this story was worth all the beatings in the world, it was even more powerful. It best marked the rejection of the daughter. We are already far from the truth, and yet fully within it. When I write, I always begin with something that I know, that I have lived, then it transforms, opens up, rambles; the "I" could become "she," but "she" is more myself than "I." "I" is a mask.

Moreover, what is it that I'm doing with you now?—Yet I'm not writing, I'm speaking.—In fact, I embroider, I put things in parentheses, I don't tell you the exact words that I heard from this man and those that I spoke, first because I have forgotten them and then because, even if I knew them by heart, they wouldn't translate the reality that I lived. My reality is that this young man attacked me and I defended myself, justified myself. That is how I experienced this instant, as an aggression in which I was the weaker. Without knowing it, he touched a sensitive spot; he asked me the question that I endlessly ask myself: "Why write books like those that I write? Is that writing?" In some way, he stripped me in front of an entire audience. And then I also found him charming. And finally, he was a man. His wife didn't say a word.

So, let's return to the story as we learned it in school: logical, with a beginning and an end, dead. I have to finish to reach what interests you, to reach the blood.

Leaving the library, I had to go to a nearby bookstore where many people had asked me to sign their books. I realized that the couple was following me. They were there at the bookstore, standing away from the crowd, silent. I don't have to tell you that I saw no one but them. I feared them and at the same time they were likable to me for the very simple reason that in France, it is rare to see a young and handsome man with a woman who isn't very pretty, although the opposite is quite common. So, I thought, "In addition to his looks, he is intelligent."

Finally he came to speak to me. We were alone, I had finished signing the books, his wife joined us. He told me that he was in analysis. You see, at the library I was so occupied with defending myself that I didn't even see his expression.

Yet the expression of neurotics is something which unsettles me when I come across it. These people are my brothers and my sisters; even more than that, they are my twins, my likenesses. I want to fight for them, to help them. Neurosis is a terrible illness, an unbearable experience; it isn't by chance that it is the origin of 95 percent of all suicides.

This young man had this groping look, this despair, this call for help, this inability to express himself that I know and understand perfectly. Something urgent. The alienation of the neurotic is tragic because it is an alienation which doesn't cause the entire world to sway from sanity to insanity. There is only you, inside, who swayed within futility, within disorder. On the outside, everything is normal, you seem to be palatable to society, while on the inside you know nothing about society. The more you sink into neurosis, the less you are able to dwell within society, and not for political or other reasons, but for reasons you don't understand, you don't know; you are handed over to an unknown which wants to hurt you and tracks you endlessly. It's hell.

The man who spoke to me in this bookstore had all of that in his eyes; if he dared to speak to me it is because he knew that I knew. He had attacked me clumsily, but this is the opposite of what he had wanted to do. It isn't easy for a neurotic to truly express himself. He is hidden behind so many defenses, so many iron plates which he created without even knowing why! So, when he begins to break through these layers which suffocate him, his communication resembles an explosion; it is often an attack.

I immediately changed my tone, I tried to help him speak, I listened to him. The events unfolded in a very friendly manner: the librarian invited everyone to come to his house for a drink. He lived in an old house in an old neighborhood. A big house with large rooms and high ceilings, full of flowers and plants. It was warm, congenial.

At the beginning of the evening, I returned to Paris, and since the couple was also returning, I took them in my car.

And there, as if by chance, I got lost. . . . I, who have such a good sense of direction! It took us two hours to get back to Paris, rather than half an hour. At each crossroads, I got lost a bit more. And during this time we talked and talked and talked. He sat at my side and she sat behind us. From the beginning he said: "I should, after all, introduce us. This is Jeanne, who is a professor of philosophy in Paris, and I am André, a professor of philosophy at X."

It startled me to know that they weren't married, and also to learn that he was a professor at X, because X is my husband's home town. It is a town where I spent some very oppressive days at the beginning of my illness. I left Algeria with my first child in my arms and fell into a sooty town in the north of France, into my in-laws' family whom I didn't know, very kind people, but very strict, very religious, adhering to principles and prejudices that were not only bourgeois, but above all Christian. I can tell you, that was a very difficult time for me.

All the memories of this time came back to me bit by bit, and it is normal that I lost my train of thought while the man spoke, and I responded a bit abruptly: "I don't need to know your name, your age, your profession, it doesn't interest me at all. . . ."

That didn't prevent us from talking.

He asked, "Would you like to have dinner with us?"

"I don't know, I must go home first." Yet I had nothing to do at home, I was entirely free that evening. If I give you all of these details, it is to give a better answer to your previous question about periods, when you said that now that I am immersed in writing, I no longer need to have periods. Since you know the conclusion of this story, I must tell you how I became lost, how I was confused, how I resisted. You will see what happens.

So here we are in Paris.

Annie: And the woman, what did she do?

Marie: Nothing, she was very discreet, very silent. I went to my house. I only went upstairs and then returned. I don't know why I did that because I was certain to have dinner with them. All of my actions were bizarre: that I lost my way on the road, that I went home for no reason, and then that I couldn't decide on a restaurant. I even said roughly, "I am not taking you to dinner. So, you must tell me how much you want to spend for a meal so I can choose a restaurant in your price range." I know very well what made me say that: I wanted to be the same as them, the same as him above all. I did not want to be a more or less well-known writer whom he admired. I wanted to be the same, equal. All of that wasn't like me. Usually I throw open the doors of my house to all who approach me, especially to those who are younger than me and ask me for help, consciously or unconsciously. I am fairly gracious, fairly maternal. That day, I refused to be like that.

With this incident involving the restaurant I was lost again. There was a blank in my head, a vacuity, rather, a freedom. I had no idea of a place where we could go. Yet I went to restaurants quite often, I knew several, of all types, expensive and inexpensive. There, all of a sudden, it was as if I didn't know a single restaurant in Paris. Finally, since they depended entirely on me because they knew nothing of this themselves, I said, "Let's go to the Rue Mouffetard, there are a lot of restaurants there, we'll certainly find one."

I like the Rue Mouffetard; it reminds me of certain streets in Bab-el-Oued or in the Casbah in Algiers: narrow, very steep, with stores, lights, and people everywhere.

I parked my car at the top of the Rue L'Epée-de-Bois, near an old theater which had been demolished and which Jean-Pierre had managed in 1968. I can say that he lived there, it was his laboratory, his drill ground, his home. People came, they brought texts, music, ideas, the plays were spontaneously born. It was interesting. I went there each day after finishing work, and I became impassioned with what went on there. I was happy. All of this corner of Paris is synonymous with happiness, creativity, and youth for me. . . .

So, here I was on the Rue Mouffetard with this couple. I wasn't trying to analyze my ramblings, to reflect on the situation. As much as I behaved in a hesitant and mistrustful manner before, I now felt myself just as unconcerned, free, cheerful.

We walked over the entire street, inspecting the posted menus and prices of each restaurant, looking into the store windows, their displays, mixing into the crowd which strolled along, came and went. There were Arab cakes in pyramids, lambs turning on spits, stuffed tomatoes and peppers. All that I love, the smell of herbs and spices. And then we found a crêperie at the top of the street, near the Place de la Contrescarpe.

Now, this restaurant wasn't absolutely unknown to

me. I had come here once with my brother, a long time ago. My brother is a man I do not know. He is older than me. The age difference which should have faded with the years hasn't faded. When I am with him, which is rare, I always feel like the not-serious little sister that I was; I fear the solemnity of my brother, his severity, his intransigence. . . .

There was a huge crowd in this crêperie, people were squeezed together around narrow tables like sardines. We found three places: he at the head of a table and she facing me. The atmosphere was casual, animated, we chatted. The waiter, a bit cramped for work space, jostled us a little, the customers got up and sat down, there was a continuous movement and clatter that isolated us. To hear each other better, this man and I drew even closer together, and we leaned toward one another. We spoke in a carefree manner, shoulder to shoulder, with our legs slightly entangled under the table. It was extremely pleasant and I have a very fond memory of it. We talked late into the evening. The woman had completely disappeared and I have no memory whatsoever of what she might have said or done. Only he and I mattered. The night was delicious. . . .

And the next day I had my period! When it had been months and months since I'd had it, and when I believed that I wouldn't have it any longer. My doctor had told me that it seemed, in fact, that I had an early menopause. It happens. Many times during the course of the evening I thought of that, of the fact that I was in menopause; each time that pinched my heart a bit. I was an old woman and he was a handsome young man. What a shame! We got along together so well.

During the night which followed this evening, I dreamed of blood, dreamed that I had my period. Since my psychoanalysis, I am always forewarned by a dream or day-dream that I will have my period. As if my body knew this well before I did. When I woke up in the morning, I thought, "It will be a bit heavy if it begins." And, in fact, it began that day.

Annie: That's a good story.

You realize that you tell me that you have made a choice in life, that you have chosen writing; and that since that time you haven't had your period, as if you no longer needed it to live, and now you evoke a little story, distinctly erotic, which as early as the next day is accompanied by your period.

I think we have to talk about that. First, because it's the most difficult subject to approach when we want to speak of our femininity, the most denied, the most repressed, and as such the most interesting. We'll find something in this, don't you think?

Marie: Perhaps. In any case, it is something that I often think of. But you see, I don't know anything, I'm looking. Quite simply, I believe that women are more unaware of their bodies than men are because of oppressive taboos which weigh heavily on our blood, our menstruation. I have felt these taboos even more strongly than normal women because I have always reacted to bodily experience through my belly. I have always transplanted the sickness in my head to my uterus. I've had all possible gynecological complications. Each time they were resolved when I resolved my psychological problems.

Annie: We see that clearly in the story which you just told and also in *Les mots pour le dire.* For you, menstruation is a crucial point of femininity, it is charged with sense; so much so that it disappears when you no longer need it. From the time that you no longer want children, nor want to have children, your periods cease, they have absolutely no purpose in making a book. But from the moment when you again find the need to make something other than a book, they return.

Marie: Yes, that's right; but I wonder if it isn't the same with all women.

Annie: I think it is the same but less clear-cut. What I mean is that women respond to menstruation as if it were the general rule of their bodies, a sort of obligation, necessity, or law that they menstruate. They respond without realizing the profound sense of menstruation, without seeing what it intimately contains of desire or refusal. It becomes nothing more than a mechanism, and women are, in general, more regular than you are. Do you see?

Marie: Yes.

Annie: But in my opinion, I'm not pinning an award on them by saying this. On the contrary. They abide by the rule of femininity that prescribes that from about twelve you menstruate, up until fifty-five, when you can stop because it isn't really the time of life to have children. During all of this, it is steady, it comes every twenty-eight days, creates a nice little machine which works well. It is the standard response of femininity. We wonder about those who fall out of this pattern; we should wonder about those who function like machines, without having embraced the phenomenon of menstruation, of its rule.

Marie: Annie, wait a minute! We're doing something distorted. We're taking my case and moving toward generality. We mustn't forget that we will perhaps use this discussion to make a book. So my case is not only particular, but in addition to that, it isn't normal. Therefore, we must support it, I believe, give it weight, say what we know from other cases that might serve to strengthen it. For example, I know that in most cases of anorexia women no longer menstruate. I know from gynecologists that many women cease menstruating after having been raped or having been left by their husbands, or after losing a child. For these same reasons other women, on the contrary, have had anarchical periods, losing blood ceaselessly, at any time, no longer having a regular cycle. What madness!

We mustn't forget, either, that there are irregularities which aren't psychosomatic, which are purely physiological.

What I mean is that the gynecological life of a woman

is closely tied to her mind. Ultimately, I even believe that we shouldn't need the pill to control whether we have or don't have children. If we better knew our bodies, I think that we would better know when we were ovulating. During this time our temperature rises and we don't feel it, while the same rise in temperature is felt if it is caused by something else.

I am thinking of the tribes which waste away or disappear, which no longer reproduce. They say it is because of consanguinity. I wonder if it isn't because it isn't possible for them to reproduce in the new conditions of life that civilization offers them; life is no longer possible under those conditions. I know it's dangerous to make zoological comparisons, we must be suspicious of it; but this doesn't keep me from thinking that the same phenomenon occurs in animals whose liberty is taken from them: generally, they no longer reproduce.

All the same, I think that we are the only female mammals that stop menstruating at a certain age. Dogs and cats, in any case, can have young for all of their lives. And the older a woman gets, the more she risks having abnormal children, children with Down's syndrome, while men's sperm doesn't alter with age.

Don't you think that there is a conflict between desire and reason, between life and death as well? Don't you think that a woman knows that there is a strong possibility that she won't be able to raise her child if she has it too late? That she prefers to have no children to having an abnormal child who will live no longer than she will? What I'm saying is serious, even scandalous in a sense. But why doesn't anyone research these questions? I'm certain that they would arrive at troubling, even startling discoveries.

Annie: Yes, we should seriously study the tie between women and their periods, how they react to this in their bodies, how they internalize this relationship, how they intimately mix the imposed norm with their own desire so that the two become, at times, inextricable. And how they must reach a point where they can adjust to both of them.

That is why this phenomenon of the period, which begins at a certain age and ends at a certain age, is certainly a mixture, the mixture of norm and desire. For example, how is it that in France, we are confirming that the mean age of puberty is decreasing. . . .

Marie: And the mean age of menopause is increasing.

Annie: That's it. They say that in other civilizations, Mediterranean civilizations, for example, women begin to menstruate much earlier for natural reasons: climatic, bio- logical. . . . But how is it that in our country, where natural conditions are always the same, we have noted, in fifty years' time, a change in the age of puberty of young girls? Is it simply that there is a sexual perception that is stronger at an earlier age, or maternal tendencies which appear earlier? What makes girls "become" women earlier?

Marie: That is, femininity, as it is experienced in our day and country, is tied to menstruation, which is, in turn, tied to sexual activity. When you don't menstruate, you aren't sexually available, either because you are too young or too old.

Annie: I would also say that it is tied to fertility.

Marie: Mostly to sexual activity. Women want to make love simply to make love. They also want to have children, but they don't consciously think of this each time they sleep with a man. They think of feeling pleasure, of orgasm.

Annie: Yes, and you are only regarded as a woman during part of your life. There is the time before femininity and there will be the time after it. What constitutes femininity isn't absolutely guaranteed; that's serious. I could not be a woman, can no longer be a woman, I am a woman only if I menstruate.

Marie: Menstruation is tied to the idea of youth. Take, for example, last year in Quebec; a group of women produced a women's play called *La nef des sorcières* [The ship of sorceresses]." There was a fantastic speech on menopause. When Luce Guilbault, the producer, looked for an actress to read this part, she couldn't find one. All the actresses who were old enough to read it wouldn't. They all gave the same reason: they couldn't imagine what it was like to be in menopause. . . . They couldn't put themselves in the character's skin. Only one dared to claim: "I have a young lover. I love him and want to keep him. . . ."

All the accepted ideas, be they cultural, aesthetic, etc., weigh terribly on our sexuality. They say that twenty is the age for love, yet each and every one of us, both men and women, knows that this isn't true. The compensation, "The best soups are made in old pots," is no help, for men don't pride themselves on it. They hide the old pots, they are ashamed of us, and that doesn't make us happy, to be treated like "old pots."

Annie: In her book on old age, Simone de Beauvoir discusses sexuality after menopause and it is truly interesting. But I would like to know how many women in menopause succeed in simply experiencing their sexual activity.

Marie: I think that that can't be a good experience unless they live with a man who doesn't really care about principles or prejudices or old ideas, who loves them as they are and continues to make love with them as before.

This doesn't prevent me from believing that a woman who no longer menstruates has problems with taking the initiative.

Annie: That is, if the occasion arises, she says yes; but if not, she has more reserve than before.

Marie: I think it can be like that.

Annie: She needs another's desire before she can consent to her own femininity.

Marie: Exactly. Menopause is a sort of shame that weighs on her, a shame that makes her desire indecent.

Menopause must mean the end of desire. All the same, the woman's lot is absurd: all their lives they must hide their blood, and yet this blood is their medal of honor, for when they are obliged to relinquish this red decoration, they are no longer women; they are children or grandmothers. In any case, taking the sexual initiative is forbidden. And God knows that women take the initiative!

Annie: With the paltry means that are left to them.

Marie: Yes, and with those means that aren't offensive, with those that we are accustomed to, that we know very well how to manipulate.

Annie: We must overflow with ingenuity, be crafty, pretend not to. . . . It's malicious. Is it fun?

Marie: It's totally perverse, totally hypocritical; it's cute as a fish hook and ravishing as fly lures for trout. . . .

I think the very fact that we know from birth that we will change our names on the day of our marriage gives us, as well as a blurred identity, the sense of a game, of duplicity, of fluidity, of flight.

Annie: Yes, women never truly know when they are women, under what conditions they are women. Certainly, there is a less strict imposition about what concerns women than there is about what concerns men.

Marie: We aren't defined in the same way as they are. There, too, the situation of the woman is absurd in our society. Women are the guardians of tradition, of education, of all that is or should be stable and they themselves can have many identities; they can change according to the fact that they are the wife of X or of Y. . . .

Annie: Even in social roles. For example, a woman may or may not work, while a man who doesn't work is an idler, and to be an idle man is far more serious than it is to be an idle woman.

Marie: To such an extent that you have terrible trouble, if you work and your husband doesn't (which is my situation), in establishing this with the tax bureau. For him, it is an inadmissible and even suspicious situation. One tax collector declared to me once, "I don't understand why you stay with him, you could divorce, that would give you a more understandable situation." When I stated that I liked it the way it was, that it didn't bother me at all, the guy gave me a funny look. I felt that he thought, "There's something fishy here."

Annie: The role of woman is a sort of navigation into the uncertain. It isn't played out at the outset. What is played out is what is imposed by the exterior: a young woman must find a husband who will give her children, etc.

But, theoretically, there is a wide range of psychological possibilities that is much greater for women than it is for men. Everything concrete is more possible for men.

I ask myself if this vague side isn't the rich side, the side which must be worked and investigated. I would say that I don't give a damn about a certain definition of the woman, and that I even want to subvert any possible definition, for to define would be to stop, would be to give an answer to something which is more or less defined, as we know, by virility. But there isn't a counterpart to give to virility, there isn't an image of woman in regard to man. On the contrary, we must show to what point we have never fit into a definition. So much so that they say we are the most contradictory things, that we are whimsical yet down to earth, that we are dreamy yet hooked on reality and on the home. I don't think that it has been good, at the beginning of the feminist movement, to try and say: here is what we are. We are the whole of all that can be, a point, that's all.

Marie: In the end, it is men who are rule bound. . . .

This vagueness pleases me, this gift of vagueness. But I would like all human beings to allow themselves to be vague; I wish that men were allowed to be vague.

Annie: Exactly. If we really work within this vagueness, we will prove that they, too, are vague. This is what interests me in the work that we can do, the books that we can write. And it will be easier for women to arrive at this conclusion because men are set in their ways, they don't know just how vague and fertile they are.

Marie: I fully agree with you, that would be the greatest service one could do for humanity; it would burst History as we live it in our civilizations, a history which labels, limits, baptizes, buries, and "chronologizes" everything. If we admitted that everything is vague, that the vague is a pleasure and comfort for the human being, it would be more interesting to live, after all. But it won't be easy to have men admit this because their rules matter to them.

At the base of it, we women are in a privileged position at this moment because we are derived from a definition that has been given to us for centuries. . . .

Annie: And that has never been properly filled out.

Marie: Evidently, because each time you define, you hinder, block, stop.

Going to Annie's house I felt a sensation comparable to that which I felt when I was a child on the road to school. In both cases I was always late. . . . It was a race against time.

I lived near the terminus of the tramway, in upper Mustapha, in the hills of Algiers. So, I could have taken one of those scrap iron insects whose antennas shot out sparks of blue and gold at each crossroads. But on the one hand, they were slower than my legs; and on the other hand they often held a formidable gentleman: André Gide.

My family lived in a large, two-story house surrounded by gardens. The upper floor was occupied by Jacques Heurgon, a professor at the university, and his wife, Anne Desjardins, the daughter of a French patron of letters. During the Nazi occupation of France, certain writers crossed the Mediterranean, and those who had been welcomed by Desjardins at the Abbey of Pontigny naturally ended up at his daughter's house in Algeria. She had three children and her house very quickly became too small. And so my mother, enchanted by this good fortune, put our house to the disposition of the "masters." Gide would come each day to lounge in our library, a small paneled room with books from ceiling to floor. He found original or deluxe editions of his works, which he would proofread with fury. He would put his flourish next to each typographical correction and would write in his journal about the inadmissible and lamentable state of the typesetting of fine editions. When he ran into my mother, this was his only subject of conversation. He was fanatical and I hated him.

Once a week, the Heurgons went away. I no longer know where they went. As Gide didn't want to go with them, I was asked to prepare fried eggs for his lunch. This only happened two or three times, but it seemed to me that it happened often, I had such a bad memory of it. First of all, I was paralyzed by the admiration and respect with which the world surrounded him; and then I was twelve or thirteen and wasn't particularly talented at cooking. At the specified time, I would go to the Heurgon's kitchen where Gide waited for me, sitting on a chair near the stove. The ordeal began. All of my movements were spied and commented upon by Gide; how I broke the eggs, how I let them fall into the bowl, how I put in the salt, the pepper, how the heat was too high or not high enough. . . . He only had to do it himself!

That didn't mean that this good gentleman didn't intrigue me, for my mother had forbidden me to open his books: "They aren't for little girls." It goes without saying that

I opened them the first chance I got and I didn't understand a thing in them. My curiosity had been sharpened and, as he often received guests in the salon of our house, I decided to attend one of these get-togethers clandestinely, thinking that I would hear lewd talk. A corner of the room was occupied by a grand piano draped with a shawl from Seville which fell to the floor; this would be my hiding place. One day, returning from class, I began by making a good snack; then, having secured these provisions, I hid myself under the piano, knowing that I would be there until late in the evening. From behind the fringe of the shawl I saw very serious men arrive, among them Saint-Exupéry, whom I had seen other times and whom I liked because he had a little round head at the top of a large body, always in uniform.

I was bored that day just as I am bored today by the gatherings of Paris intellectuals! It was interminable and it didn't help me understand my mother's prohibition. . . .

Apart from that, Gide had often looked at my books and my Greek and Latin notebooks and, by asking wicked questions, verified that I knew nothing. Indeed, these investigations often took place in the tram. As this was at the end of the tram line, often just the two of us were there at the outset. It was impossible to avoid him. There I was, in my uniform of the girl-from a-good-family-who-goes-to-a-good-school with my satchel, doing my homework on my knees at the last moment. He arrived in his cape and beret, with his Chinese head and his tire tread sandals. I was scared stiff.

This was a major reason not to take the tram. What is more, I knew a very quick route, a sloped and perilous shortcut which had the advantage of making me cross Galland Park, my paradise. Paradise first because it carried my Aunt Lilia's name, a big and generous woman whom I loved; and next because on its slopes it had trees, plants, colors, smells that I loved. I ran at top speed, I flew as if I

were an airplane over patches of green, red, yellow, over
smells of freesia, of wisteria, pinks, roses, and jasmine. I was
so sensitive to all of that, yet I didn't have time to look
because my attention was drawn to the steep slope that I
descended, where the slightest wrong step would have
caused a dangerous fall. I jumped to avoid a rock, but that
didn't stop me from smelling that the tea roses were flow-
ering, that the cypress tree's shade was denser, that it had
rained the night before.... This path gave me a great feeling
of exaltation, my entire being was occupied with it and I
enjoyed it all the more when I imagined the tramway creep-
ing along through its toils and probably shaking Old Man
Gide in a clashing uproar. So much for the sparks!

To go to Annie's house, there is no tram, no Gide, no
Galland Park, no smells or African colors; there is only what
is necessary: a pleasant and absorbing haste.

But above all, on my way to Annie's house, there is the
little alley where I went year after year, week after week, to be
cured, to become a part of the world. Going to the meeting
that Annie arranged for me, when I had time to do it, I slowed
down and considered the narrow passage in this neighborhood as a whole. When I didn't have time, my soul went that
way while I continued to drive without having an accident.
Each time I drove by, I saw the woman that I used to be
approach the gate of the last house on the left. Each time I
drove by, I felt a love for this woman whose body carried me
twenty, thirty years, love and tenderness. Each time I drove
by, I thought of the agony which made me hurry over the
broken pavement.

How could I think of agony so simply, on a beautiful
morning, as if I were thinking of a lunch menu! How could I
evoke it without the fear of having it come into being and of
feeling it strangle me? From where did the strength to conquer it come, to deliver the trembling woman from it?

Unchangeable. The world must congeal. This fixedness is necessary to block the rise of fear. The woman struggled to escape the throes of agony which presently, surreptitiously, clung to her, without her having been able to foresee the attack. The woman was restless; she thought, "It's nothing, it's nothing. It will pass," while the sweat already soaked her body and her heart beat quickly. It sufficed to stop everything, to dig herself into a dim, smooth, silent place. To drive everything out, to do away with it all. For agony clings to anything, to bits of light in a sunbeam, to the chirping of the birds in the square far away, to the metallic noise of the pail that someone throws down in the courtyard below. It clings to even less than that, to the quality of the light which tells the time of day, to the air which blows under the door indicating the weather, to the smells of space between objects which reveal life. What life? What does it mean, to live? I can't live! It's necessary to obstruct even more, to paralyze everything, annihilate everything. Unchangeability. Statue. Minerva in a walkway of groomed boxwoods, whose white eyes never blink, whom nothing touches, who feels neither rain nor wind nor the gaze of passers-by. Especially not the gaze of others. Faceted eyes, glistening, peremptory, murdering, deceitful. Swords. Daggers. Pitchforks. Knives. Armaments of terror. Flames of horror.

The woman burned from the outside. She was at the center of the cataclysm which embraced the universe, which ravaged the town, the country, the continents, their children.

Close the eyes, mouth, ears, nose. Do not move, curl yourself up, wall yourself in. So that the outside no longer exists.

Submarine. To be an armored submarine, blind, lying on a sandy beach of great depth, where nothing moves. Dead.

All the pain that agony takes to present death, this immense actress which is white, mauve, gray, and rigid on the stage of immobility!

Death was the only way to reach peace. Which death? The razor blade, the revolver, a fall into space, pills, gas, the metro, the river, the rope . . .? Which one of these toboggans would most easily slide the woman into death?

There was a sort of delay while the woman looked for the best way to conquer the restlessness, the movement, change. She felt as if she were choosing her suicide; this gave her importance, as before, when she went to market and said to herself, "Let's see, what's good, not too expensive, and will make everyone happy at home: pork, fish, eggs . . .?"

This repose doesn't last, it is only a landing on the staircase of agony. Now the inside of the woman begins to stir. The door of death slammed shut because the woman saw her dead body, the body that she herself had killed, offered to the stares of others. No! Not death!

She is a prisoner of herself, of her blood, her excrement, her sweat, urine, tears, saliva, of her digestion. Cells die and are replaced, the heart beats, the blood circulates, what I eat turns to shit, what I drink turns to piss! Everything moves! Why? All will continue to move in death. Putrefaction. Decomposition. Fermentation. My black flesh stinks. My blood runs on the sidewalk, across the cracks in the cement. My stomach is so swollen with water that it can explode. My gray cadaver is at the morgue, waiting to be delivered to a man or to children. No! Not that!

The woman runs like a crazy person! She flees!

I spoke and I set her free. I fought for years to free her and I did. She sleeps within me now, with my youth. She is safe, calm. Finally.

I don't leave her. I was born from her little by little. I emerged from her quietly, while, curled up like a fetus on the doctor's sofa, she searched out the words which would utterly destroy the agony. The larger I became, the smaller she became. I began to walk. One day I was strong enough to take her inside of me. She was only a minuscule embryo, a seed of childhood, a seed of hope, a seed of love. A beginning. I was nearly forty. I haven't lived very long.

It did me good to pass the doctor's street with the house at its end: I stirred up memories and measured precisely the incredibly long distance that there is between the woman that I was and the woman that I am. We don't belong to the same galaxy. But my wealth lies in having been this woman, in now being the woman that I am, and in being able to pass between one and the other; for the bridge which unites us is solid: it is the minute analysis that I did, three times a week for seven years, of what plunged me into neurosis. I stripped away all of the laws that served to tear me to shreds.

Laws of class that, for the love of my mother, I never judged, never shaped to myself, even less rejected. I shouldered their severity, hypocrisy, and pomp without contesting them. They formed a yoke around me which tortured me to insanity. Bourgeois rules are bad for humans, they debase them.

Next, laws of men which are laws of all powers. Women only have the power to trick, to lie, to adjust.

The laws of the Catholic Church, which mix the two preceding laws in a vile amalgamation painted in colors of sacrifice, war and gold: our morality.

The submissive one and the rebel. But my submission and my revolt are not carved from the same wood. One was blind and the other had a lynx's eye. One is made of hollow words, the other is made of words full to bursting.

Speech is an act. Words are objects. Invisible, impalpable, revealing boxcars in the train of phrases. Men hermetically sealed these words, imprisoned women within them. Women must open them if they want to survive. It is an enormous, dangerous, and revolutionary task that we undertake. These are the very words that I write. I am not afraid of the noun, nor am I afraid of its adjectives. I even claim that we must open the words "task" and "revolution" to find within them the desire and the game from which they have been separated.

Annie: If you were to speak of your writing, would you classify it as game, joy, or struggle?

Marie: Joy and struggle are entirely mixed, completely overlapping one another when I write. For example, right now I am writing a book in which Ireland—a certain corner of Ireland—is very important; it is even the theme of the book. I must describe a bit of the coast, an inlet. This description is imperative, it sets the tone of the book; I have to bring out at the same time both the flexibility of this place and its permanence, for these two elements are the key to the story. To be able to translate this countryside into written words, I begin to do battle with myself, I must plunge into my desire and know exactly what it includes. Only a perfect interior accord, a perfect honesty, can make me move on to the act of writing. It is a very destructive struggle that I lead within myself. When my desire doesn't give way to analyzing, I take up my notebook and my bic pen and try to write.

I never make it on the first try. I use similar strategies to those that I used in my childhood when someone forced me to eat something I didn't like. I used to say to myself, "a-one, a-two, a-three and go! Purge." I swallowed everything whole. I do a little of the same thing with my pen. I force myself to write. I write, "I have nothing to write. Why? Because I don't know how to write. . . ." Like that for five or six lines and then, little by little, I take off. It's a process of kicking myself in the ass. Finally, by virtue of working, of fighting with myself, I begin to find the opening which lets my thoughts flow, and then it becomes a game, a wonderful game. Once I've embarked upon a page, I can stay with it eight or ten hours at a time, which are the best hours of my life; I have no other needs, I'm happy, I don't pay attention to time, I'm neither hungry nor thirsty, neither hot nor cold. But before living these hours, what torment, what wasted time! Let's say that it takes me about three years to write a book, and in these three years there are six productive months. Six months during which it flows, it matures, nothing can stop me, not even my most destructive reflections about what I'm writing, about writing itself, about my pretension to be a writer. A few delicious months and the rest of the time I cut myself to pieces, make chop suey out of myself. . . .

The struggle of me against myself. Sometimes I destroy myself, I can't write for weeks. I'm ashamed of my vanity. What possesses me? Who do I think I am?

Annie: And whom do you accuse yourself of being?

Marie: Someone who has the nerve to be published,

that is to give pages that come out of your own head, just like that, to thousands of other people to read. What pretentiousness! I'm paralyzed by the claims and the importance that I give myself. I find the elements which made up my neurosis once again, the desire to cut myself down, a bad conscience, self-hatred. . . . But my desire to write is so great that it can work past that.

Annie: That's because in that, you exist.

Marie: Yes. I still dream that I was born to perform in a cabaret.

Annie: How's that?

Marie: I would have loved to be Yvette Guilbert who sang and spoke on stage. I had this opportunity when I was a student. I belonged to an amateur theater group at the University of Algiers. We staged *Monsieur de Pourceaugnac* by Molière. An official from the Youth and Sports Ministry saw the production and asked us to participate in a workshop in Avignon. I went without telling my parents. To play in amateur theater with students was all right. But to go wandering around France with people from the theater, that could never be allowed. I had decided to separate myself from my family that year, to distance myself a bit, because I was beginning to suffocate.

It was the beginning of the festival. Gérard Philipe played *Le Cid* and *The Prince of Homburg;* he was beauty and kindness incarnate, and we admired and venerated him. We stayed in Lourmarin, which is a wonderful village. The program kept us busy all day, and in the evening we would hitchhike to either Avignon or Aix-en-Provence! What liberty! I didn't know how to profit from it, I always felt guilty. Yet one evening, in Aix, I attended a performance of *The Abduction from the Seraglio,* and I was amazed by it. It was presented in the courtyard of the archbishop's residence, the night was warm, full of stars, and in the pauses in the music you could hear crickets by the thousands, slicing through the surrounding obscurity. It was beautiful. It smelled of the Mediterranean.

I have to say that I met Jean-Pierre for the first time at Lourmarin; he was the assistant stage manager. That was more than twenty five years ago. . . . We were twenty.

In the course of this workshop we staged a show and decided to prepare another that we could take on tour upon our return to Algeria. It was to be a Prévert-Cosma musical, with songs and poems.

There, I was caught up in a sort of huge wave that distanced me from my family very quickly. Too quickly. I wasn't ready. We went to Paris via youth hostels and we asked Lili Cosma, Cosma's wife, to come and watch us and give us advice. She was a small blonde woman who had taken first prize in the piano competition at the Berlin Conservatory. She came, she made us sing scales one after the other: do, re, mi . . ., and she kept three of us, two men and myself. She took a great interest in me; to such an extent that I stayed with her in Paris, on the Rue de l'Université. Cosma was cheating on her, he didn't live there; Lili experienced that dramatically. In a way, she used me as bait to draw Cosma to her house. Because Juliette Greco had become famous, she sang songs other than Cosma's. They were looking for someone to replace her. Lili thought that by making me work at it she could make me sing correctly. So, all morning I worked with her, and in the afternoon Cosma came to hear me. He was there, Lili was happy, and I was terrified: it was a daily exam. Lili organized everything. She had me audition at the theater in the Latin Quarter where Michel de Ré directed. She had me meet Rougeul, who was with the Rose Rouge. The deal was in the bag: I was going to do my tour in Algeria, then I would return to Paris to sing in the evenings.

I was attracted and frightened by this universe which was so far from that of my family. My family was relatively cultivated, we had a box at the opera and seats at the theater, but to pass from this to the other side of the stage. . . . Actors and comedians were people who weren't serious and who did fairly un-Christian things in their homes.

I couldn't choose. I put up a terrible fight against the enterprises of Lili. I hid behind my mother, saying that she would never let me do that. I hid behind my studies, claiming that I had a diploma to get and it wasn't like me to leave things unfinished. It was then that Lili decided to come to Algiers to persuade my family; she would follow the tour as its accompanist. . . . It was dreadful. My family looked at this little blonde woman, a German Jew, as if she were crazy. To go on tour with students, at her age! She wasn't normal. Especially since she brought a lexicon in her bags and insisted on teaching the household servants the alphabet. . . . She followed them with A's and B's and Z's, and Bahia, the chambermaid, signaled to me right under the ringlets of my elderly friend that she was insane!

I was incapable of deciding, incapable of rejecting the principles and prejudices that filled my head and that I had convinced myself were good because they came from my parents.

But during the short period of time when I sang and recited poetry on stage, I was very happy. I felt a great pleasure in discovering the audience, in seducing it, in finding the rhythm of the evening. I instinctively knew when to move from a song to a poem, how to unite moments. I felt the smallest vibrations of the room. No two evenings were ever the same. Each time I had to adapt to a different audience, which very quickly became one single person whom I had to attract, who had to like me, with whom I wanted to communicate. It went well, but I let it go. Added to the stage fright which is normally felt was an insupportable agony, that of betraying my mother. . . .

Annie: So you didn't become this cabaret woman that you should have been, which would have made you happy; you became a writer.

Marie: Before becoming a writer I was the woman that I had to be, the woman that I had been prepared to be by my education and upbringing. I was a mother, a wife, a housekeeper, and all of those for a long time.

Annie: Is there something that writing and the cabaret have in common?

Marie: I told you, I perform dreadful surgery on myself when I write, and in the cabaret it's the same. But the distance isn't the same. In the cabaret the audience is quite close, and you find it or you don't find it in only a few minutes' time. With a book, the distance between you and your audience is immense. You do your work alone for years; and once the book is published, you only meet your audience if you don't have much success. If you do succeed, you don't even know who that audience is. In the cabaret there is always an echo. With a book, you can never have the slightest echo. Nothing is arranged so that the writer meets the audience, nothing. It's hard to take.

No writer can honestly deny the importance of the reader. When you take a manuscript to an editor, you know what that means; that means, "Give this to the public." If not, you would keep it in a drawer at home. But there are nuances in the way that a writer thinks about his public. There are those who lay books like chickens lay eggs, standardized, ready for consumption, regularly, and his audience is made up of clients; he is a writer in the same sense that one is a tradesman.

There is also the writer who searches and who knows that he won't reach a large audience, it isn't a question of trade for him; but his small audience is attentive, demanding, dangerous, fanatical, and it drives the writer's quest from book to book; the audience is indispensable for him.

Finally, there is the writer like me, who is neither tradesman nor specialist. This type looks for an audience and, more often than not, never meets it. But occasionally she finds it, which is my case. The meeting is both passionate and

agonizing because it is precarious. When you aren't a trades-
man-writer, when you don't serve books à la carte, you
always run the risk of deceiving your audience and losing it,
the risk of finding the deaf and dumb universe of the writer
who doesn't sell, for there is always trade between those who
write and those who read. It's unbearable.

The agony doesn't only come from the possible loss of
the audience, that is loss of communication with the outside;
it also comes, for me, from the fear that I must play the whore,
that is, do whatever is necessary to keep my readers and so
become a writer-tradesman. If that happened, I would no
longer have any respect for myself. So I constantly live on the
razor's edge because I need others as much as I need myself.

The problem is to bury myself deeply enough within
myself to find the simple core that I want to write, which is at
once my own and is a part of everyone.

I fear hermeticism, that is, a road over which few
readers can pass because it belongs to me alone. I don't fear
it because of solitude, but because of the pretentiousness that
it implies. I don't like myself well enough to invite just anyone
to meet me, Marie Cardinal. In my books I think that readers
meet a woman who lives in France today, and who basically
resembles all women. That is who I am.

I know the magic of hermeticism; I saw it during my
psychoanalysis and I understand that some choose this way;
but I didn't choose it. I chose the other way, the way of the
crowd of people. I can tell you why I made this choice; but first
I want to tell you about the dialogue, at once secret, totally
satisfying, and sometimes very poetic, that can develop between the patient and his analyst.

There are people who often say to me, "Because it is
only a question of talking to yourself, I don't understand why
you need a doctor. You can get along without him." That was
what I, myself, thought before; it seems that I knew all about
introspection.

I began my analysis without believing in it. It was only a pause before returning to psychiatry. At the beginning, my words came out as usual. It took me a few months of sessions to realize that I was talking like a parrot, that I was more "lived" than "living," that the words I spoke belonged to my family, my social status, my upbringing, not to me. It is the invisible and silent presence of the doctor which made me aware of that, because it is there; it is only noticed in the clearing of his throat, or in his movement in the chair. That is enough. He never judges, never comments, never directs, but you feel that he is attentive, very attentive. At first, you pay attention to what you, yourself, are saying and you find that there are words in speech which appear like hairs in a bowl of soup and others that don't fade. In other words, speech becomes alive, that is the beginning. After that, you get used to making associations and establishing relationships between moments, memories, and thoughts which you never would have thought of bringing together. It is the words which serve as vehicles, which lead you to find other words: identical-words, synonym-words, mirror-words, enemy-words. These words really become key words; and, as the analysis gradually unfolds, they allow a rapid and profound communication between the analyst and the patient. And even if this communication is silent on the part of the doctor, you still know that it is complete. It manifests itself in a very intimate, hermetic dialogue. These words are, therefore, so many syntheses of long and important sections of the analysis, which themselves comprise pertinent bits of the very life of the person who is speaking. For example, if I meet with my analyst and I say to him, "The dog is in the universe of the refrigerator," I am certain that he will understand what I mean. For someone else to understand, I would have to write thousands of pages or talk for hundreds of hours.

I like the speed and esoterism of hermeticism, the warmth you find there when you know its keys, this fellowship. Yet I haven't chosen this way to express myself. I've chosen the complete opposite.

Why have I made this choice?

It's simple.

In my childhood, then in my adolescence, I received a maximum of information, words, the entire gamut of signs protected western women use to recognize themselves, to get by with, to profit from the world. All that caused me to go mad, as you know. I swallowed it wrong.

Later, history and my will cut me off decisively from the universe of my childhood: France lost Algeria, my mother died as well as my grandmother, and I decided to burn all the bridges between me and my past. On top of it all, my husband's job required him to live outside of France.

So I became a woman who had three children to raise and not a cent in her pocket. My illness prevented me from practicing the well-paying job that my diplomas could have secured. My children and I lived on my small part-time jobs: minor secretarial work, proofreading, documentation, journalism; I could do these at home, for the most part. That lasted seventeen years. Seventeen years in shit, in penury. I didn't work on a whim or on a caprice or for distraction. I worked to survive and to feed my children. I had terrible financial difficulties. I swear that I knew the cost of kilowatts, steak, sweaters, and shoes for children's feet that never seemed to stop growing. I felt the rent go up just as the measles set in (writers got social security benefits beginning only on 1 January 1977 . . .) and the gas was turned off. I waited in the interminable lines in the administration buildings where they give average French women a bit of aid, provided that they fill out innumerable forms and come one, two, one hundred times to windows where they are often received as coldly as a dog in a bowling alley.

But I didn't live all of that as if I were an average French woman. First of all because I had chosen to be one, and second because my experience gave me escapes that aren't available to the average woman. Music, painting, reading, the simple fact that I could stroll around Paris dreaming of lines, rhythms, sounds. . . . There are free days at the museum and reduced "family prices" for attending exhibitions and concerts where you can get in for almost nothing, or free. On certain days I was happier than I had ever been during my lucky bourgeois days. I had never looked at paintings or listened to music as I did at that time.

The problems which usually limit women who live in the same conditions as I did heightened my capacity to dream. The women that I met in the school yard or in the shops, my neighbors, those who taught me, little by little, how to cope with mediocrity in the same way that my mother taught me how to cope with fortune, couldn't share in my "cultural enjoyment." From birth I had a treasure that they couldn't even imagine. The colorless, uniform strand which strung their days together was the ribbon of misery. They borrowed their dreams from Charlot's films or programs by Guy Lux. It is all they were given.

These women touch me; I wish they could read my books, and I swear that I think of them when I write.

Annie: Do you think that there is something specific, something important that happens to them?

Marie: Yes, I think so. You see, I accept all the invitations that I get from small rural groups, from libraries, plant workers, committees. This year, I traveled outside of Paris once or twice a week and went all over France. There is an invigorating rebirth of feminine consciousness in our society. Much more is happening than you might think, but it goes on in the background, in secret, and it is difficult to explain at the moment.

Annie: Do you think that this is something that has touched the lives of all women?

Marie: No, not yet. But that is coming. Not long ago I went to a home for young women laborers in Beauvais and to

Istres to speak to a group of women between thirty-five and fifty who were mothers of blue collar families and, having already worked, were now housewives trying to become "home help." These meetings impassioned me because I felt that these women knew about real problems but didn't know how to express what they understood; they didn't have the vocabulary, the contacts, and that made them powerless. But they are beginning to realize what is wrong.

Annie: Why do you approach these women? You don't go to earn money or to shine in the eyes of the public, so why do you do it?

Marie: Each time I feel that I am meeting real people. Having lived with them for a long time, I know the kind of contact that they have with the stuff of life, with the bodies of their children, with the seasons, with duration; and it is real contact. If you aren't in full contact with your actions, you can't possibly wash dirty clothes well, gut a chicken well, scrub toilets satisfactorily, fully care for a child, or buy cheap but well. These women know all about life, death, freedom and love, but they don't know how to express it. First of all, they aren't used to doing it, it isn't their place, it's a man's place; second, they don't have the words to do it.

Through these meetings I can find once more the essential universe of women from which I have withdrawn, now that my books sell. I give them my knowledge and I show them that we can give ourselves the right to talk about everything and not just about the subjects that have been reserved for women up until now.

Annie: It's an exchange.

Marie: Yes, for me it is an important exchange. I am heavily imprinted by the seventeen years during which I slaved like a madwoman just to survive. I feel closer to the women with whom I shared these years than I do to any other women. When I think of someone reading me, I want to write for them.

There comes a time when the manuscript is finished; when the mass of papers that I wrote, corrected, reworked one after the other for years forms a whole. The last line of text was enough to make a manuscript or perhaps a book out of this pile of typed pages that I know perfectly, whose first pages are already yellowed and dog-eared from having been read and re-read, handled too roughly, exposed to the daylight more than the others.

I reached this goal some time ago. The words, commas, accents, and white spaces are stuck together like caramel candies in a humid candy jar and begin to form a block independent from me, outside of me; it is a block that has an existence different from mine, even though I participated in each one of its signs. It is very similar to a child.

There is something poignant, quivering, serious in the delivery of a book, as there is in the delivery of a child. An intimacy, a promiscuity that will end. A fear of what will be after, yet the desire to no longer live in the before or in the present. Curiosity. The feeling that something irresistible is beginning to form, that the cell divides. Life splits in two. How are we, who are still only one, going to live separately? A false unity made out of our two independences, the work's and mine. A future inflated by my life and the eyes of readers. An explosion of our inseparable solitudes.

You, like a plateau which rises in more or less white layers, depending on where the paper was purchased; with your misplaced w's that are lazy and get caught by the following letter because they rarely fall beneath my fingers; with your corrections of all colors and thicknesses: huge black, little green, peremptory red, blind blue, and even smudged pencil. And me, like a goat attached to your picket, like a dog in your corner, incapable of withdrawing from you, even if I go away for three days, leaving you to rest in your gray cloak on the table; even if twenty people are carousing in the house; even if I am making love in the bed at your side. You, like a voyeur, a jealous lover, a demanding husband. You, in my dreams, my plate, my bath, my kisses, in my streets.

You, like an abandoned wife, pregnant with my forgotten desire, powerless, unable to live, paralyzed with distress because I don't know what to do with you, because you weigh too much, because I no longer believe in you. Me, the vagabond of doubt, wandering through the nights of others, drinking their books in huge gulps, their talent in choking mouthfuls. Disowning you, disowning myself. Deceiving you like a coward.

But the recognitions.
But the insane happiness.
But the perfect harmony.
But the power.

All of that to separate us compulsorily, necessarily; because the gestation is finished. It would kill us to stay together.

I lived in a mad passion for the final six months of gestating *Les mots pour le dire*. The untitled manuscript and I were of one flesh. We would fall asleep, spent, body against body. Each morning I would wake with my head on the pages, my left arm embracing it, protecting it, a pencil in my right hand. Just the time needed for my consciousness to climb to the surface of my half-opened eyes. A few seconds. I saw it. And my heart picked up the rhythm of our love. My body didn't have time to come back to life, my arm still enclosed it, my head still rested upon it, yet my eyes looked for its words, its lines, its last paragraph.

I'd set out again for ten, twelve, eighteen hours. All day alone together in passion. As if it were my lover or I were its lover; as if it were my child or I were its child. Entangled, embroiled. At times, two stubborn beings set one against the other. Me, unfaithful, wanting to mix a life other than its own into it. It, like a wall in front of me, refusing another word.

There was only my dog Bonnie to tear me from this union. I heard the little clicks that her claws made on the parquet of the empty house. She came to see where I was. Her instinct warned her that I was busy. So, she went off to her corner where she laid back down with a great sigh. Finally, her strategy exasperated me. I didn't like this distraction, or what it implied: I had to leave to take Bonnie outside!

Outside, I profited from this interruption to do some necessary errands in the emptiest store. Then I sat on the most isolated bench on the avenue and watched my dog do her duty. The time that she took to sniff the sparse grass! What care she took to choose the spot to go! What trivialities! That provoked me even more because I inevitably thought of me and my writing. Hours circling a few words! Yet it was so easy to say what I wanted to say. To say. But not to write. How could I imprint my beloved manuscript with the eloquent mimics of the body and face that accompany speech? With the silences, the tone, and the musicality of the voice, the look charged with unexpressed yet understood words, the hands, like trays of fruit full of silent phrases? Ultimately, how could I imprint this manuscript with all of the traits of speech which charge words with the exact sense that you want to give them?

Annie: You are a story teller.

Marie: Yes, that's tied to my childhood, it's Mediterranean. You know that the Arabs are wonderful story tellers as well as wonderful listeners. They get together in the squares of towns and villages to tell and listen to stories. They sit in a circle, in groups, leaving an open space in the center, as if it were from this void that the dream would rise, and they tell stories in turn—anyone who wants to tell a story.

When I was little, there was a woman like that on the farm. She told half-Arab, half-French stories. I will never forget them. Stories of winged horses, serpents crawling through tombs, of men Allah seized by the hair.... I will never forget the words, but also her gestures, her eyes, the smell which came from her cooking fire, the bumpiness of the trampled earth beneath my buttocks, and the mysterious corners of her shack, lit only by the daylight that entered through the low door.

I like that, to speak, to seduce people, to enchant them, convince them, stay with them. The warmth of words in these instances! Their weight! Their juices, secrets! To exchange them for attention!

Annie: Isn't there also a desire within you to bring

something, to give something? You said the other day that you liked teaching.

Marie: Yes, but it is the exchange that was important to me in teaching.

I never could pass the *agrégation* exam because I had three children in four years and each time one arrived, it was at the time of the examination. You can't do both at the same time. So I have a *licence* in philosophy, but I have only been a lecturer because a professorship in philosophy is held by someone who has passed the *agrégation* exam.

My first teaching position was in Greece, in Salonika, and my first course dealt with relative pronouns! At that time, I went to all kinds of trouble to learn grammar. When I was young, grammar didn't interest me. I blundered through it, learning by heart just as much as was necessary to pass from one class to the next and put my diploma in my pocket. What interested me was math. And then I did philosophy to please my family. . . .

So I learned French in order to teach, and above all by teaching it. At times, I wrote big mistakes on the blackboard, false rules. That caused a wave of murmurs in the class and it didn't agree with the exercises in the book. I had to say, "Listen, I made a mistake, let's start again." Because I had a good rapport with my students, this worked well. I remember that I really knew something when my students understood. And in the end, we learned together. I am convinced that when you like to exchange, you can learn or teach anything. I think I would be able to teach Chinese!

Annie: Perhaps that would be a good lesson: to communicate things the moment they are learned, as they are learned.

Marie: When I meet the women who ask me to speak with them, I don't at all go with the idea that I am going to teach them something, but with the idea that we are going to exchange something, our lives, our reflections, our experiences.

Annie: What is important in the exchange, why is it interesting?

Marie: It enriches, there is a warmth, a love that flows.

Annie: You recognize each other.

Marie: Yes.

Scraps. Shreds.

Something unusual happens when I attempt to write this book, in which Annie takes the humble role of cultivator as well as the important role of locomotive or midwife.

Our conversations have been recorded by a tape recorder, then transcribed onto paper by a secretary. One hundred and eighty-two pages of words exchanged in complete freedom, loosely. And also the voids of what hasn't been recorded because I pushed the wrong button.

Usually, nothing limits me when I write. Here, I was limited by these one hundred and eighty-two pages, by what they contained and what they didn't contain. Our petrified words incessantly mix with those that aren't petrified, mix with that which will become written, spoken, or silence. Our words had been absurdly paralyzed by machines, fixed in space and time; while that which beats like blood, that which is most alive, is that which doesn't exist.

So we have the unrecorded story of the delivery of my manuscript. A story that I have tried to write for some pages now, in vain, because writing is free; it transports me far from these one hundred and eighty-two pages. The story digresses from the general, recorded passage in which I speak of the women who touch me, of the reader that I want to join . . . a love story.

The vague and the rule bound.

Where was I in it?

It began with "There comes a time when the manuscript is finished. . . ."

Yes, my beloved manuscript was finished. I even

found a name for it. And one day, late in the afternoon, I took it to my publisher in its pretty bound covering with its metal clasp. I left it on a director's desk, in the hands of strangers. Good riddance!

Then I came home and slept for twelve hours.

The next morning, the moment that I woke, I realized that the manuscript was no longer there, open to the last page. No more pencil in my hand. No more feeling of the paper against my cheek.

It is finished, at the publisher, it walks alone.

Satisfaction, at first, as if I had taken a difficult exam and had passed (I knew that the editor would take it). Contentment for a work seen through to the end. The rows upon rows of knitting have become a real sweater that keeps you warm. The furrows upon furrows of hard labor have created a field where wheat grows in green darts.

Then an emptiness. Like the silence of a country railway station after the agitation and uproar of the heavy travel hours. Stability. The unusual resonance of tiny noises: chirping birds, the buzz of a bee, the breath of the station master. The stop. The station. Won't there be any more movement? Do I know how to live in this calm? Vertigo. Is falling into this repose like dying? Will I travel again?

Vacation, finally. I have worked hard. Now I am going to have fun. I am going to relax. I am going to do things that I like.

What, for example?

For example, some good food. I love to cook when I have the time. Something that the family relishes. For example, a leg of mutton with a potato puree. A leg of mutton which I will buy from my Arab butcher who sells lamb that smells like lamb; not this sweetish, whitish lamb that the French eat. A rich and garlicky lamb. And a potato puree that isn't too stiff and not too liquid, beaten a long time with a fork. The kids call that "mou-mousse" puree, because my family calls me Moussia. And as an appetizer? Hard boiled eggs with mayonnaise. That's quick. Everyone likes it. And for dessert? I'll buy a tart from the baker, who makes them much better than I do. I'm not going to make too much fuss. So what if it's more expensive, for once.

Suddenly something crossed my mind. Something so strong that I sat on the bed and stayed there with my back straight and my legs pulled against my chest, crushed: for whom am I going to make this Pantagruelian meal? For whom? For my children? But my children are gone. How stupid I am! Could I have been able to work so well if they had been here? My children are grown, they're no longer at home.

I didn't want to see the danger right away and I thought of occupying myself more than of relaxing. I wanted to put something in the place of the manuscript. Do some work.

Perhaps I could rearrange the hall cupboard! For six months, I drew laundry from that cupboard, which I filled with packages from the launderer; I slit them open and took out sheets, towels, or dish cloths as I needed them. After six months, this formed a magma of rags, of papers, mixed with slips of shredded transparent plastic packing. This didn't at all resemble the linen closets of my youth, those attics filled with embroidery, those reservoirs of yarn and stacked lawn, those strong boxes which smelled of lavender when you opened them, full of white, regular columns of sheets.

Yes, that's it, I'm going to rearrange the hall cupboard. Take everything out, clean everything, put paper on the shelves, put sheets with the sheets, pillow cases with the pillow cases. . . .

What time is it?

Half past six.

For the fifteen years that I have been writing, I have become accustomed to rising very early, so as to give myself the most time possible before the children woke at seven. For fifteen years, I have seen the night of winter mornings, the dawn of summer mornings. Now, the children are no longer in school; they aren't even here. But it is stronger than I am. I have kept the habit of beginning my day at dawn.

Half past six. It is useless to get up at half past six to arrange the hall cupboard, I have the entire morning ahead of me. I can go back to sleep, read, do anything.

At a quarter of seven I am standing in the living room and am seriously vacuuming the rug. These hairs that Bonnie leaves are a curse! You have to go over them again and again to get them. With a move of my wrist I have to bend the brush of the hand tool so that it reduces the opening through which the air comes; that creates a rupture, a kind of break in the flow of air which often picks up the hair and draws it into the machine. It isn't hard, but it takes time and it must be done. If not, the hairs form incredibly hard little balls which, under the pressure of shoe soles, wear the rug. It's amazing how matter attacks other bits of matter, how concrete walls themselves will deteriorate rapidly if you don't care for them! Children don't understand that. No matter how often you say it, it's pointless. I repeat often enough that disorder and dirt are luxuries we can't afford!

What am I doing with all of these banalities! What am I doing worrying about Bonnie's hairs this morning! Who is going to walk on them at seven, at eight! When will someone walk on them?

I turned off the vacuum, I stood up, I had a long, useless hose in my hand. Useless.

Ten minutes later I was in the street. I fled the house. Useless. Empty. No one.

Who is empty? Who is useless? Who is no one? The house is empty, useless, no one? And that's why I'm crying?

Huge, heavy, profound tears, which come from somewhere unknown, very wet tears to water the morning sidewalks of my neighborhood. How stupid it is. What purpose does it serve?

I am empty, useless, no one. I cry over the procession of the morning, over unfinished breakfasts; over Bénédicte, who was the last to leave, always late, with her pretty Scottish skirt that I bought at Galeries Lafayette and lengthened as much as I could. I cry over Alice with her pretty face sobered because she never knew her lessons and the anguish overtook her at the last minute; she would hold back. "You see what happens when you put things off. . . ." I cry over Benoît, who was always too warm and would leave in his shirt sleeves during the heavy frosts of February, the sleeves of his anorak dragging along the ground, his torn satchel letting rulers, erasers, all of his material escape: "This is the last time that I'm sewing this and you won't get another one, young man. . . ."

I cry over an overwhelming time, and minutes too short. Hurry, soak the socks, I'll wash them this evening. Quickly, the linoleum in the kitchen. Hurry, the bed. Hurry, do the morning shopping, bread, milk, so that they have something for lunch. Hurry, I'm going to be late again. Shit.

Hurry. Hurry. Hurry. This evening. . . . Later. . . . Tomorrow. . . . Sunday. . . . The markets, the dishes, the washings, the potato peelings, the mendings, Alice's silences, Bénédicte's whinings, Benoît's squabbles. Hurry. Hurry. Hurry. Sixth grade. Junior year. Meetings with other students' parents. Clothes. The iron. Heavy cleaning, walls and ceilings, once a year. All the same, it's better than when they were little: naps, bottles. . . .

Time passes quickly! Twenty-two years! At this pace, it passes quickly.

I cry over my arms, my hands, my body, all empty and useless. I cry over my half loaf of bread when I used to need two. Over the piece of ham that added to my baskets, which already weighed eight to ten kilos each. Over my underwear and bra that needed washing, even though there was already washing filling the sink. And over the strength you needed in your back to lift all of that wet laundry.

I cried. I even sobbed. The baker's wife appeared in her door, ready to chat. I liked to exchange a few words with her in the morning; she was very young, very neat, plump and pink. Her peroxide blonde curls were hair-sprayed into an immovable scaffolding above her pert features, both joking and sensible. Her husband, when he heard us talking, often came and planted himself in the doorway. He was bare chested, in light work pants with old shoes on his feet, vigorous and young like her, the power of his hairy chest and arms still dusted with flour. He never chatted; it wasn't his role.

The baker's wife saw my face and, disturbed, she went back into the shop.

How could I tell her what was upsetting me? She wouldn't have understood. It wasn't my solitude, my uselessness which made me cry. My manuscript had so absorbed me that I hadn't even seen my children as they left home. It is even thanks to their absence that I could write as I never had. A manuscript; I was going to begin another soon. I will be consoled soon.

I cried for women. Yes, for women's lives. I had never seen so clearly the absurdity of their existence as it is annulled by custom. Not only were their labors, hardships and sacrifices abolished one day; it was the essential which was destroyed; the wisdom that constant contact with matter gives to women; the knowledge that the daily use of substance gives to them; the intuition of life and death assured by their persistent relationship with the body, theirs, their husbands', their childrens'; all of that denied!

They live in submission, in resignation. To protect themselves from nothingness and give their lives meaning, they unconsciously develop a detestable possessiveness, wretchedly gripping those they have served all of their lives. Meaning. How would they dare speak of what they know? The words to say it, the true words, words at the beginning, of birth, are all shameful, ugly, unclean, taboo. For their profound intelligence comes from blood, feces, milk, mucus, earth, sweat and skin, juices and fever. They don't know how to explain how all that ties into what they essentially know: happiness, liberty, justice. They don't know how to translate the knowledge of their bodies: the length of gestation, fertile viscosity, nourishing bulk, the danger of fermentation, the necessity of mutation, the weight of time, uncontrollable space, the precariousness of limits . . . the archaism of our lives as women.

I want to write for them. I want to give them words that will be arms.

Annie: When writing is marked as women's writing, "That is a woman's book," isn't this always a way for men to feel that they need not be concerned with what we tell them? Yet we are persuaded that what we tell them concerns them too, that it is addressed to them and that they should confront it. It shouldn't be a question of women's books, but of a book by a woman.

Marie: I don't think that there is a masculine or feminine writing. But I do believe that there is a difference in reading according to whether the words were written by a man or a woman. Knowing or feeling this, women who want to be understood (by men as well as by women who have tried to resemble men) have, consciously or unconsciously, taken up the practice of masking, making up, preparing their writing. To adapt themselves to the great concepts, the great thoughts, the big words, women often ornament all of these with adjectives, commentaries and explanations, as if to excuse themselves, as if to reduce these immensities (habitually manipulated by men) to a woman's size. Moreover, they follow this same explicative procedure when they want, on the contrary, to give value to the "little words" of their universe. This occasionally produces writings that are ornate, full of imagery, showy, with tinsel and ruffles, jewels and disguises; they are immediately stigmatized by agents, slapped with labels like "ravishing," "charming," "intelligent," "sensual," or even "learned"; but they are also labeled as not having the brutal and simple force of the classic men's works. . . .

When you refuse to excuse yourself, when you use no subterfuge and use words as they are, use all words, then the critic warns the public that you don't lay it on thick, that you don't do things in grand style, that you are aggressive, an exhibitionist. They talk about the performance and the phenomenon, they no longer talk about the writing.

When Gisèle Halimi discovered how Jamila Boupacha had been treated by paratroopers in Algeria, she decided to tell about it publicly. So she and Simone de Beauvoir wrote a report in which it was mentioned, among other things, how Jamila Boupacha, a virgin, had been raped by soldiers who forced a bottle into her vagina. The article was sent to *Le Monde*. The paper's response came quickly: "We will publish your article in full. However, you must change the word 'vagina'; it isn't attractive and it doesn't fit the paper's style. Find something else." Simone de Beauvoir and Gisèle, subjugated as well as obligated, changed the word. The article

appeared and *Le Monde*'s readers could read, one fine afternoon, that Jamila Boupacha had been raped by soldiers who
had forced a bottle into her "insides." Gisèle is still outraged
when she tells this story.

Right now, for those of us who write, there is a huge
problem: our language, written or spoken, is never received
as we want it to be, as it is.

Annie: That's why you were disappointed when *Les
mots pour le dire* was received as a book about psychoanalysis. Yet it isn't a book about psychoanalysis, but a book about
the adventure that develops during psychoanalysis, an adventure that develops during words.

Marie: Yes, that's right.

Annie: It's reading that has been shifted entirely. It is
changed according to biased interests which are ultimately
theoretical. Yet it's really a question of something else all
together. What is serious is that this is the very snare of people
who read. They don't even know how they are caught. They
believe that they are captured by a reflection on psychoanalysis while they are really captured by the intimacy of an
adventure which grips them.

Marie: That is, whether conscious of it or not, readers
are conditioned by agents and the media, who are often
terribly sectarian, commanding, self-concerned and back-
ward.

A reading of my novel is warped for two reasons:
first, it is easy to read; second, it is written by a woman.
According to the norms of French culture, these two elements cannot, in principle, go with the gravity of the treated
subject: the life of a human being, true life. It is clear that
serious questions arise; it is a question of life and death,
dream and happiness and politics. All of that in a novel
written by a woman which reads easily? No. So it's neither a
novel nor an essay, it's a document about psychoanalysis. It
isn't literature, it's a testimony.

When the book began to sell, it was classified in *L'Express*'s best-seller list under the section entitled "Fiction." Then, when it actually became a best-seller, it moved into the same paper's section marked "Non-Fiction," where it stayed in second place for over twenty weeks. Why the change? I would like to know why.

Then they say, "It's not a novel, it's an autobiography." As if all novels weren't autobiographies! As if hiding behind the third person to write, or changing sex, or escaping into dream and the fantastic isn't as revealing, as close to confession and intimacy, finally as close to autobiography as a story written in the first person. I know nothing more than my own life, and I don't want to write in a voice other than the first person. I need to be the woman in each one of my books. I have been the six women of my six books, some of which are written in the third person; and as I hope to write at least twenty books, you will be able to say that I wrote twenty autobiographies. . . .

Tournier's book, *Les météores,* came out at about the same time as my last book. It's a magnificent ode to homosexuality, to excrement, and the anus. The critics received it as the fine book that it really is. They spoke about it in terms of literature; they didn't dwell on the way that Tournier reveled in shit, filth. He is permitted to do this because, although he is homosexual, he is, after all, a man. He has a penis, that's what you need.

I'm not saying that my book has an equal, superior or inferior literary interest to Tournier's book. I really don't care and I don't compare. I'm only saying that my book has a literary interest, but this was never considered. I think that's because it enters into subjects taboo for women, like shit, for example. It is for this reason that I talk about Tournier's book.

What a fuss over a few pages! Not even twenty pages! A Parisian critic, who had read the manuscript for Grasset, said to me with regard to the passage where the dead drunk mother goes to the bathroom on herself, and where I used a word like "shit" or "crap," I don't remember which:

"You mustn't use these words, we can't have it."

"But what words do you want me to use? I've used the words of our language."

"You could say discharge, for example."

No! Not "discharge!" I refuse to use these hypocritical flourishes! Women know better than men do what shit is, if only because it is the barometer of their children's health. They know all of its textures, colors, odors. Why is it coura- geous and strong when men talk about it but shameful when women talk about it? Why? Excrement is excrement, and if I have to write about it, I use the words which will translate it into my own language, which is French. Period.

Annie: Something similar happened with *Parole de femme* [Woman's word]. The critics often discussed it as a theoretical work, they only saw it in its theoretical dimension. I wanted that, but something else did enter into the book: I wanted to write. They take it as a basket of ideas, but not as the work of a writer, not as a written work.

Marie: That's irritating. Even more so because they seem to lay claim to the "literary" dimension while I, person- ally, don't like the word "literary" as it is understood in France today. I don't like books to belong to a specific genre. I like them to be at once novel, poetry, essay, research, history, philosophy. I want them to recognize that I write, even if I don't write classic women's work or so-called "women's novels." I don't want them to say that I testify. You don't have to be a writer to testify. But I am a writer.

To say that I'm a writer is something! It's at once pretentious and a treason: pretentious because the writer is seen by the public as a mythic character (and God knows that I'm not mythic, that I'm made of skin and bone); and a treason because a writer is construed as masculine (and God knows that I've the buttocks, breasts, and sex of a woman!). But I refuse to use a word other than writer because it is the only one that will do, for the moment, to describe a person whose most important occupation is writing. So I use it and I consider this use combat. "Writer," like "Literary," is a word to open, to make larger, to revive. I believe that critics and readers must get used to letting us use words as they are, without adding to them or digging out a feminine, or even less a feminist "touch" when it's we women who use them. If we win this war, we can then invent words to stop up the empty spaces left in our language by immense unexpressed and essential domains which are all, as if by chance, feminine domains. Domains which, moreover, belong to humanity; paying attention to these domains must necessarily enrich everyone, men as well as women.

Right now, every word has two senses, two sexes, according to their use by a woman or a man. All words, except technical words; but if you want to, we can talk about those later.

Let's take a word like "table." When a woman simply writes "table" in a common sentence, for example, "there was a table in the room . . .," one reads this table as if it were spread, clean, useful, waxed, adorned with flowers or dusty. When a man writes, "there was a table in the room . . .," one reads this table as if it were made of wood or some other material, the work of a craftsman or laborer, the product of work, the place where you go to sit and eat or talk. This word lives differently according to whether it was written by a man or a woman. Now take a word like "Liberty," for example; the distance between the meanings of this word written or spoken by a woman and written or spoken by a man is dizzying. A woman who isn't a self-declared militant or a specialist in this type of question must explain what she wants to say when she writes "Liberty" if she doesn't want this liberty to be taken as license. When a man writes "Liberty," he doesn't have to define it; his word is immediately understood as liberty. The

"I want to be free" of a woman doesn't have the beauty and grandeur of the "I want to be free" of a man; she can use these words, but she must explain herself. All of the principles and prejudices that weigh on us are found in the words that we use, without our realizing that the same principles and prejudices forbid us to use certain other words.

Annie: That means that we must define what we put behind our writing, behind our words; if not, we know that they will be understood differently, we always risk being out of place or misunderstood.

Marie: In effect, that is what we would have to do so that our writing remains in the ghetto that it is in today, so that it continues to be criticized and read as it is. Personally, I begin to find that there are enough of these pointless formalities and I think that we don't have to define what is behind our words, but use them as they are, without doctoring them. For those of us who write, the difficulty is to use the totality of the material which is at our disposal, without taking forbidden usages into account, without adapting our words, without creating another ghetto—that of a "feminine writing." We already know what a woman poet, doctor, or lawyer is worth . . . not a straw. A woman writer is hardly worth more. It isn't a question of creating little squabbles in a clique; it is a question of leading a veritable combat, a struggle, as united in sisterhood as possible, but firmly.

The best way to prove that words are lacking, that French isn't made for women, is to put ourselves in close proximity with our bodies, to express the unexpressed and to use the French vocabulary as it is, directly, without cleaning it up. It will thus become evident and clear that there are things that we can't translate into words. How do we describe our sex, gestation as it is lived, time, the duration of women? We must invent. The language will become more feminine, it will open up, be embellished and enriched. Our sisterhood will be fertile and welcoming because our words will be useful to everyone.

Annie: Let's take Hélène Cixous. I truly think that she writes from her very flesh, without trying to respond to any demands, without entering into language as it is, coded, imposed. . . . But she risks being forgotten. Moreover, she's almost always forgotten and almost always not understood.

That is what is difficult, if one wants to simultaneously write without cheating and be read. I wonder if there isn't always some form of compromise in writing. . . . If I write the word "love" I'll surely be obliged to write what I mean by it, because I don't want anyone to understand it to mean exclusive love or a single and absolute passion. . . .

Marie: Or legs waving in the air among cornflowers. . . .

Annie: I certainly don't want anyone to understand it as that; so I can't simply say "love." I'll have to write an entire book to say "love."

Marie: You don't need to explain. Who would these explanations be for? For those who don't want to imagine that there is another type of writing or language? Let it be. Once the first scare has passed, the public won't misunderstand; especially women, who want to express themselves more and more, who seek out their own "births," sometimes with an unbelievable avidity.

The danger lies in justifying yourself, in explaining. I think that we must write brutally and disrespectfully.

Danger also lies in technical, scientific, or specialized language. When a woman uses this kind of language, she has every chance of being taken seriously. She doesn't have to worry about being understood, in a manner of speaking. . . . Here's a sentence: "Because to speak of ideology is to cause a fundamental relativity of accepted discourse and to pose it as hindered in regard to its own causality" (Catherine Clément, *Miroirs du sujet* [Mirrors of the subject]). A woman wrote this, but had it been a man, this would have been the same, it would be read in the same manner. Technical words have no sex. They have no scars or histories, they offer no prize; and most often, they haven't had time to live. They are neuter.

These words serve as a mask to those who use them, men and women alike.

Annie: There, I think, you're mistaken. Thinkers, philosophers present themselves as such, not as writers.

Marie: Why aren't they satisfied being published by specialized presses? Why go to Gallimard, Le Seuil, Grasset, etc.? In doing that, they reveal their desire to reach a greater public than that of the specialized presses, whereas their writing is incomprehensible for the majority of the public.

Annie: Yes, there's truth in that. When Kant wrote his *Critique of Pure Reason,* he didn't think of the public, he thought of philosophers. And it's true that French thinkers today have a desire to reach people other than the specialists. Yet they should realize that they still don't reach anyone but the "specialists."

Marie: I think this is a dramatic situation, something poignant. What do traditional philosophers do? They leave it to the care of second-rank people, or people they consider second-rank, to popularize their thought. They form an elite, an aristocracy, a little, exclusive universe of privileged people. What do the philosophers whom we spoke of earlier do, the ones who publish in places other than reviews and specialized editions? They seem to want to directly transmit their thought without going through the popularizers. You might say that they want to communicate. And yet they don't succeed; they don't establish that communication. Their thought is still clear, even bright at times; but the words that carry that thought are obscure, absolutely unintelligible. What does that hide, how do we interpret this unsuccessful act?

Do you realize what would happen in France if millions of people could really read the books of Foucault, who is by far the easiest to read? (I say really read because I know that *L'anti-œdipe* by Deleuze sold twenty or forty thousand copies, but how many really read it, and how many bought it solely out of snobbishness?) Do you realize the upheaval that would cause among people who were disenchanted, neurotic, at the limits of despair? Do you realize what a stimulus that would give them? They are stuck in the mire of an old, hereafter unthinkable thought, while another kind of thought already exists, is already debated, already opened up! But they don't know it, no one told them! Even if someone had told them, they wouldn't be able to understand the words which carry that thought.

It's wrong to say that these words are the words of the future and in time we'll learn them. I claim that these are technical, specialized words, the words of an elite; some of these words will leave the domain of scholars, but most of them will remain there. What is dramatic is that we believe these thinkers are using difficult concepts because the words themselves are difficult. We are led to believe that when it really isn't true.

One day at a gathering I heard Bernard Noël declare: "An unreadable book is a censored book." This sentence amazed me. I began to think of all forms of censorship. First, legal censorship. There are laws that exist in France which warrant the power to get rid of certain books. And then the most visible: commercial censorship, which provides that a book is purely and simply not published or that it is mutilated because it isn't salable. Next, cultural censorship: because of a lack of familiarity, because of the lack of a rich vocabulary, there are books you can't understand which are inaccessible treasures. Finally, there is internal censorship, that which the writer turns against himself so that he doesn't unmask himself.

To return to our thinkers, it is evident that they are victims of cultural censorship. The system of education in France is such that it doesn't teach you how to live, to travel, to understand, to read in today's world. Here we produce specialists, workers, Frenchmen for 1950!

You teach, I've taught, I suppose that you agree with me when I say that the policies of national education in the universities pull the strings and hold the cocktail parties for the society of men of letters.

But above all I want to speak about the internal censorship which promotes the use of technical language precisely because it is neuter. Not only do the words themselves have no sex, but they let nothing pass from the body of those who use them. I note that Barthes, Deleuze and Foucault are all homosexuals. I would like to know how they live their homosexuality. One of them, I don't know which, forbade the publication of a work in which his homosexuality was mentioned. Why did that bother him? Why are Foucault's books easier and easier to read? (What a difference between *L'Archéologie du savoir* and *La Volonté de savoir!*) I read, or rather try to read, books by Dollé (published by Grasset), Poulantzas (published by Le Seuil), and I ask myself: What are their problems? What are they hiding? Where is their uneasiness? What does it mean that these publications are put out by nonspecialized Parisian presses? Are they so afraid of their bodies that they no longer have voices? What are the real words that they hide behind those of their science?

I also think of the people in Quebec that I know well. For sixteen years I have gone to Quebec each summer. I like the people and their language. They have a difficult time situating themselves in the world. They are pulled in pieces by the Americans, the French, and the English. They are fierce and proud. They want to live a life that is right for them, but which life? Where is it? I notice that in the publications of their presses, the use of technical vocabulary breaks all records. For example, this commentary was written in a simple weekly television guide (distributed with the Sunday newspaper, which has a wide circulation); it was intended to introduce a program entitled "The Kids are Crazy": "Religious authority and its corollary, religious submission, re-

main in hidden conflict in the motivation and psychological
texture of nearly every character. . . ." Why? So that we take a
program whose title was too close to life seriously? To mask
the true material of the program?

On the other hand, I think of Jean Genet, who told
me last week that he opposed the fact that more than five
thousand copies of *Journal du voleur* were printed. I don't
have to tell you that that made my mind go "tilt." Why? Genet
knows he amuses me, so he answered by dodging the question; the final evasion meant: maybe I don't want many
people to enter into my intimacies, particularly into that
which is in *Journal du voleur.*

It's that Genet himself is easy to read. Anyone can get
hold of him through his books, can "touch" him. . . .

I think, too, of one of my friends. He is thirty, a
philosophy professor, and tortured by an obsessive neurosis.
He is haunted by faucets, switches, and meters. He suffers
because of it. He began psychoanalysis a short time ago. He
expresses himself like a philosophy book. The other day he
spoke to me about the "game" that is played in the course of
the sessions, of the "immanence of the game in technical
analysis. . . ."

"When you speak of a game, what game are you
thinking of?"

"I think of a ludic action which is substituted for an
actual conflicting state. . . ."

"I'm asking you to name a game for me. What did you
play when you were little?"

He looked at me with irritation, always my stupid
questions! I insisted: "Tell me the name of a game right now,
without reflecting, without choosing."

"Anything at all: cops and robbers."

Just as these words left his mouth, I saw astonishment
and joy in his face: actually, his father was a cop. . . .

You know, all that I tell you about technical or specialized language hasn't come up by accident. I think of women's language. When I write, I constantly feel myself pinched by narrow vocabulary, either because I don't have the words or because the French words are so invested with meaning by men that they betray me when I, a woman, use them.

So what can I do? Certainly it's tempting to feminize language, and I know that many women want to take this path. Having carefully reflected, I don't want that. It seems to me that this would be to create a new alienation by creating a new specialized language. There would be the language of women just as there is the language of prisoners, sportsmen, priests. . . . It would be a language to use between ourselves. I am not enough of a feminist for that to interest me. As for me, I don't give a damn about the power of women. What I want is equality, justice, sharing. But I want that very strongly.

Frankly, to be a writer, a word that is considered masculine, doesn't bother me at all. I would even say that as we are at this point, I prefer that to being a "feminine writer." On the other hand, what bothers me a great deal is to have only one word to define my sex: cunt. It bothers me not to have a single word to write about my sense of time, which is very different from that of a man; the time of a woman is always present, always included in my life, ruled by periods, cut into slices by fertility. Not a single word to translate my passage of time; for I believe that women don't have the same sense of the passage of time as men; women know how to live gestation from inside themselves.

Don't you find it symptomatic that the good films by women are considered "slow" films? I think of *India Song,* of *Jeanne Dielman,* of the films by Yanick Bellon. I myself wouldn't say that they are slow; however, how do you say that their slowness is teeming? There is a rhythm in slowness, in that which is becoming, that we know and that men do not know. What are the words to express that?

Gap. Opening. Night. False night. . . . What word will make my cunt exist? What word would express its inertness, simultaneously active and somber. A hole. A well. A steamer. A sleeve. . . . To explain the sweetness of its dampness, the depth of its abyss? Footpath. Gully. Vagina. Stem. To explain the carmine road of sexual pleasure, for the child. And the commonplace story of the blood? The bloody sex?

Where is Annie leading me?
I was born when I was forty knowing how to speak

French and able to say it. Everything is new. I am new. I have just left a black and interminable underworld where I was terribly alone. I am happy to meet others, finally. I want to express what I felt, what I perceived in the course of my illness. I must speak; I must write. Before, I lived for a long time in intense terror which didn't leave me. Fear of the condition of being human. Fear of the absurdity which that represented. Fear of a universal nonsense in which I was totally entangled. Incapacity to attach reason, or what I believed to be the foundations of reason, to the universe, to that which surrounded me: people, things, all the rest. Fear of death and fear of life which held death's seed.

Marie: About death: a young friend from Quebec stayed with me some time ago. It was the first time that she had visited Europe and she was only familiar with the American way of life. One day, she was on the balcony of my apartment. (I live in a large apartment and my balcony looks out over a small square with other buildings situated around it.) That day, there was a hearse parked in the square. Louise noticed it and asked if the chauffeur who drove it lived in one of the buildings.

"No, I don't think so. It's only a hearse that has come to pick up a body for burial."

"A body in the building? You can have a dead person in this building?"

"Of course."

She immediately went back into the house; she was troubled and didn't dare to understand.

"But how. . . . You can die in a building. But can you keep dead bodies here?"

"Yes."

I explained to her that death was drawn out in France, that they kept the bodies at least three days; yet in Algeria, because of the heat, the law requires that they remove the dead within twenty-four hours.

The girl couldn't get over it. She was completely astounded. Where she came from, in the half hour that follows a person's death, if by chance that person has died at home and not at the hospital, she is taken surreptitiously to a funeral home. There, she is made up, straightened, dressed, even embalmed, etc.

For example, Yvon, one of my daughter's friends, told me about the procedure at the death of his grandmother. Yvon is from a very poor family. He has aunts and uncles who don't know how to read or write, who had been taught to sign their names only for paperwork. They had always lived in misery. (And I feel that misery in North America, among its skyscrapers, Cadillacs, and well-kept lawns, is even worse than it is elsewhere.) What is more, this poor unhappy woman, the grandmother, had had twenty-one children. Can you imagine! So, she dies. The family gets together to make contributions and pays ten dollars for a crepe paper dress and cardboard shoes that are decent, furnished by the funeral home. They also pay to have her made up and to have her hair done up in an impressive, dowager's style. With the result that there the old woman was, dead and stretched out like she had never been during her life: an honorable old woman who rests peacefully. The entire family comes, drinks Coca-Cola, eats chips, chats, plays as if the grandmother weren't dead, as if she were taking a nap. There are some that they place in rocking chairs. My husband saw an old woman that had been seated in an armchair with her knitting. . . .

That is acceptable in capitalism. When you live in this type of system, as do Americans, the only reason to exist is the possession of material goods, of money. In these conditions, death is unacceptable. So, you deny it. You are ashamed of it; the poor are even more ashamed of dying than others: because they are poor, they haven't known how to live.

You know, in Los Angeles, I think, there is a place where millionaires have themselves frozen as soon as they

die. I believe that Walt Disney and Onassis are there. The day
that they find the cure for their cause of death, they will warm
them, attend to them, and bring them to life. It's a radical
negation of death.

A capitalist ideology, a capitalist economy, can only
cut people off from dream, imagination, the universe, and the
cosmos. You struggle to possess the most that you possibly
can, you're only a robot for making cash.

Annie: In fact, by turning us away from death, by
cutting us off from death, we are taken away from life.

Have you seen death at close hand? Have you ob-
served it as it exists around you?

Marie: During the entire duration of my illness, the
terror of death never left me. I was in constant contact with it;
I saw only death, lived only with death. And that lasted for
years. I know this type of death by heart. But it was a neurotic
death, incomprehensible, unacceptable, like that of the
Americans. Not only did this death never leave me, but along
with it I was haunted by thoughts of suicide.

Besides that, I saw people die during the war. My
mother directed a unit for the wounded in a military hospital
in Algiers. At the time of the landing at Elbe and that of the
campaign in Italy, the wounded soldiers came by plane directly from the battlefield, still covered with their clotted
blood and mud.

Because the town was too small to accommodate all of
the staff, they requisitioned the schools for the troops. I
remember that my school was temporarily moved into a
church's crypt, where classes were given in large, vaulted
and somber rooms that were rare and folkloric; it created a
huge disorder, and nobody cared about anything.

My mother didn't like this liberty, the fact that I had
nothing to do. Even more so because she was busy during the
day in the hospital and couldn't watch over me. So, she
decided to take me with her. "All of the nurses have gone to

the front and there isn't much help. You can help soldiers who can't eat by themselves. We'll teach you how to shave them and how to prepare simple dressings." In fact, she did teach me to do all of that. I shared the morning with her; first, six o'clock mass, and then the hospital until the evening, where there was always more work than we could manage. I liked that. What I liked the most was the contact with the men.

Annie: How old were you?

Marie: I was very young. . . . About thirteen. But I was already a big kid; I was already one meter, seventy centimeters tall, I had developed breasts, really like the girls who live along the Mediterranean, who develop very quickly. I was dressed like a nurse and the men knew that I was young, but they never dreamed that I was only a child. It was very hot and they were all lined up like rows of onions on their beds, nude, with their wounds, some of which were very serious. They liked me a lot and I liked them as well.

When I think that my mother was afraid to see me go out of the house, but that she closed me up all day with hundreds of men who weren't wearing a stitch of clothing. . . .

I saw men die there. Their deaths didn't resemble the death that I was familiar with in my illness. They were calm, they didn't die in terror. They died solemnly, with a sort of austerity on their faces. You were acutely aware that they were in the process of living through a very important moment, but I never saw one of them feel fear, or rather, what I later called fear: agony.

I believe that death doesn't cause fear when it comes, because it is natural and you never enter death until you have accepted it. It doesn't come up by chance, it doesn't come as a surprise. It appears and only takes us at the instant that we deem it necessary and good. It isn't agonizing. Suffering is sometimes frightening, as is the aggressor who wants to kill, but not death itself.

Annie: I believe that, too.

Marie: For me, my grandmother's death was exemplary and it gave me something to think about. She was eighty-five but, in spite of that, she was never old. She had never been old. She was witty, she was interested in everything, and above all, she loved to laugh.

Alice Cécile Berthe Honorine Berger de Talbiac was born 8 November 1878, in the heart of the Algerian countryside in the big bed of a big room in a big house guarded by big walls. When she was two, her father died. When she was eight, she lost her grandfather who, by dying, left her his enormous fortune. The old man feared that, once alone, his widow would remarry and add the family goods to her dowry. So, he decided that all of his vineyards, his orange groves, olive groves, land, buildings, and roads would belong to his granddaughter, a blond-haired, blue-eyed child with a pink complexion, dotted with freckles. Her face wasn't beautiful, but lively and charming, lighted with gaiety and boldness.

When the grandfather felt his death approaching, he asked to have Alice brought to him so that he could tell her of his serious decision concerning her succession, and in order to warn her of the responsibilities that would fall onto her shoulders. She, at eight years of age, would become the sovereign; her own mother would depend on her. Then he asked her to kiss him. Little Alice complied; she had to climb up onto the bed, which was almost as tall as she was. And there, on sheets marked by the marquis's crown, she gave her last kiss to the man who made her rich. The old man let the child kiss him and then, in a gesture of tenderness and possession, put his arms around his heir. He had a spasm and then died, squeezing his arms so tightly that the child was trapped within them, crushed against the henceforth immobile chest of her grandfather. Alice didn't have enough air to breathe, certainly not enough to call for help. She had to remain like that, half suffocated, until someone came into the

room and saved her, with exclamations and sobs. The fear
that she felt had been so strong that she began to menstruate
that very evening. At eight!

The next day, the fear had subsided and the child had
become a woman. A free, independent woman who had a
taste for happiness and no taste whatsoever for business.

When she died at eighty-five, she had completely
squandered the considerable fortune of her grandfather; she
had only her husband's small pension on which to live. Her
husband was a man whom she met at a ball given by the
government and whose principal occupation, from the day
that he married Alice, consisted of helping his young wife
spend her billions. She said, "I wouldn't have married just
anyone. I wanted a husband who had a certain type of nose.
One evening I met this nose and I married the man behind it.
That was your grandfather. I loved him madly until he died."

During the last years of her life, she no longer had the
money to keep a chambermaid. Because she had trouble
getting dressed by herself, first because she had never done it
herself and more so because she was handicapped by rheu-
matism, she decided to cut the front of all of her clothes
open—bras, underwear, and corsets included—and to have
buttons and button holes sewn onto them. That way, she
wouldn't have to depend on anyone for help.

In church, on the day of her burial, I heard the priest
pray, "Lord, here is your servant Alice who comes before you.
We ask that you take her into heaven." And that made me
chuckle, because Alice said, to challenge her daughter (my
mother) who practiced her religion avidly, "Heaven must
certainly be boring! Can you see yourself playing the banjo all
day in the company of saints?"

They buried her in France's frozen ground in February. Disheveled palm fronds sprang up from the mass of
wreaths that lay in a heap upon her grave. You might have
said it looked like a palm tree that had been blasted by

lightning. It was absurd, but it was also appropriate, because in her final days she never stopped repeating, "Old age, at the point where I am in it, isn't tolerable. It's too degrading."

Marie: I'm certain that my grandmother felt death and that she accepted it. She became serious. I saw her distance herself from us for three days. She said, "Don't kiss me anymore; I don't want to feel." She continued to live very normally, eating with us, watching television. . . . But the more time that passed, the more apparent it became that she was sinking into an initiation. The morning of the fourth day, she got up very early and washed, did her hair, her make up, dressed precisely. She put on perfume. My mother asked her, "What is wrong with you? It's barely five o'clock in the morning." She responded, "I know what I'm doing. There is nothing uglier than old dead people." Then she went to bed and she died.

I've heard about or seen other deaths that were similar. I believe that death only comes when one is capable of accepting it. When I say things like that sometimes people are shocked because they think of the deaths of young people or of accidental deaths. But even in these cases, I think that there is an instant, even if it is only a bit of a second, where one faces death and accepts it; where one feels the necessity to settle into it.

Annie: I agree strongly with what you say. I've had this same experience in a car. I saw death coming. I thought of the others; I felt a great sadness for one moment on their part, then I felt very calm. I said to myself, "Well, it's now."

More and more we're separated from death. The first death that you see, the first corpse, is something terrible precisely because we are separated from it. I think that in smaller societies where young people are constantly confronted with the elderly, where they experience death at a very young age, the first death is irretrievable from their memory. Do you remember the first death that you experienced?

Marie: Yes. And again, I'm fortunate to have been born where I was. In my homeland, Algeria, death is not at all taken in the same manner by the Muslims as it is by the Europeans. They don't put the body in a coffin. They simply put it on a plank and cover it with a cloth through which the outline of the body is clearly visible.

Annie: Does it cover the face?

Marie: It covers everything, but you can see perfectly well the feet at the bottom which raise the sheet. If it's a heavy-set person, you see the bulging stomach. You see the form of the head. Only men carry the dead. They take up a rapid step when walking, sort of a lively stamping which makes the body jiggle a bit above their heads. The women scream, sob, claw at their faces; they are, for the most part, professional mourners. It's a great and tragic ceremony, a sort of dramatic festival with colors, noises, movements, music. It has nothing of the passive side, the resigned and subdued side of our funerals. It doesn't emphasize the absurdity, as ours, but emphasizes life as it is.

Those were the first deaths of my childhood. After that, when I was an adolescent, I saw a dead person: a young woman had died in childbirth. The child had died as well. They dressed her in her wedding dress and laid her one-hour-old child next to her. It was an appalling staging. I don't know why I felt that the living had retrieved these two dead people and I thought that it was ridiculous. It didn't move me.

Death only affected me from the time that I became openly neurotic. It took on a sense that it never had before. It took on an absurd sense that I hadn't felt in my childhood.

Besides, children don't generally undergo death in the same way that we undergo it. Perhaps that is because they are still very close to birth.

We make a great fuss over death but don't make such a fuss over birth. Birth must have been a terrific jumble, the passage from water into air, warmth into cold, night into light, the finite into the infinite. I've always been shocked by the expressions of panic in newborns when sleep overtakes them. You see their little arms grow longer and longer, unfolding, and then suddenly, as if this emptiness made them afraid, they quickly draw their arms into their bodies, elbows to the body and fists clenched, like they were in the woman's womb.

Annie: There certainly is an agony even more terrible than any agony of death in this reaction.

Marie: I don't think that the word "agony" is appropriate. It must have been a difficult passage, an upheaval, an ordeal. I think that agony is tied to our societies. At the moment of birth, you aren't yet a part of these societies. In spite of what you could feel during the time in the uterus, the noises, movements, the nervousness of civilized people, you are not yet a part of society. We must be able to speak of fear, even of terror, but not of agony. We certainly lived through our births with a great intensity, a great consideration, a great curiosity; but I don't think that there was already agony.

It is implausible that we don't speak more about birth, or that we only speak of it in such a stupid, delicate, simple manner. It must be something to discover, in the space of a few seconds, such things as weight, thickness, space, the glow of lights, the jar of noise, cold, the insecurity of being nude, that air doesn't cover you like water does, especially cold air.

I really had the opposite experience, once, the experience of death. I had a miscarriage with a sudden, brutal hemorrhage. Suddenly, blood began to flow from me in a steady stream. I saw it flow without stopping, without stopping, nothing could stop it. It was terrifying. They rushed me to the hospital. When I arrived, I had almost no blood pressure. They couldn't operate on me until I had regained a bit of strength. The doctors and nurses fought for my life for several hours. They thought I was going to die and they called Jean-Pierre into the operating room. I had always been perfectly lucid and, from a certain moment on, I was extremely happy. I no longer felt my body, but I felt a marvelous intellectual agility. I was very attentive to everyone who surrounded me. It was in Canada. I watched the people work with an admirable, professional tenacity. They did everything they could to save this stranger. I was a life in their eyes. I loved them because they gave so much love, so much power, and so much competence. I wanted to help them, to thank them. The next day the doctor said to me, "It's thanks to you that we came out of that; you cooperated quite well." Yet I was physically incapable of doing anything; I was completely bloodless, I had no strength whatsoever. I remember that I couldn't even lift my head. I know that I didn't do what little I did to get out of that situation because I felt perfectly well; I did it to give them what they were giving me. I was attached to a sort of raised tube full of mercury that constantly indicated my blood pressure. I saw that this column stayed between zero and two in spite of the transfusions—they gave me a transfusion of five liters. That's a lot. I was bothered a great deal for them by the fact that I wasn't doing better. That episode remains one of the most beautiful memories of my life. I no longer felt anything. I had no weight. My body weighed nothing. I had the feeling of total liberty.

Annie: You didn't even think, "I'm going to die"?

Marie: Oh yes! But that made absolutely no difference to me. Jean-Pierre and I talked about the children and decided what was going to happen to them; they were very young, the youngest wasn't even two. I couldn't see him with three children, the eldest only six, staying in this country where we had just arrived and knew no one, with a new job that kept him very busy. So we decided to entrust them to his oldest sister for a while, until he organized himself. The operation table was high enough for him to put his chin near my face when he sat on a kind of stool.

Annie: And how was he?

Marie: Afterward, he told me that he was completely overwhelmed, if only because of the blood that seemed to be everywhere, on the walls, the floor, everywhere. But I didn't realize that he was so distressed; he is a guy who really knows how to keep his composure. He didn't talk much, but let me talk. I felt absolutely wonderful, exactly as if I were swimming in warm water. I can say, without exaggerating, that it was delicious.

I understood that I was coming back to life when I began to suffer again. To give me the transfusions they had looked for veins all over my legs, my arms, and my hands. Suddenly, at about seven in the morning, I began to feel pain in all of my limbs, as if someone had beaten me unmercifully. And, moreover, because I was in a recovery room, I heard others there like me, whom the doctors tried to drag away from death. They gasped, groaned, gurgled. Yet I hadn't even heard them during the night, I didn't even suspect that they were there. Suddenly, I was afraid of their deaths; yet I had never been afraid of my own. I couldn't stand being there any longer and demanded that they move me.

We are out of touch with death. That is foolish, because life is much more interesting when you think that it also contains death.

In the end, what we call death in our world is an incomprehensible phenomenon which comes about in the lives of people raised in the west; it isn't really death. Thus, for people in the west, death in Pakistan, the Indies, or somewhere in China or the Amazon forest doesn't have the same importance or tragic significance as a death in Berlin, London, New York, or Trifouillis-les-Oies. To hear of the death of an Indian, Arab, Chinese person or Negro isn't as serious as it is to learn of the death of a German or American. Look at what is still happening today with the Eskimos, the Amazon tribes (who, by our false reasoning, are scientifically and systematically exterminated); look at what is happening in South Africa and even in Lebanon. . . . It doesn't keep the people in the west from sleeping at night. But imagine this same death in the neighborhoods of Beauvais, Manchester, or Hamburg. Whew! Each Irish death makes the headlines. If we had as much to do with each Pakistani death. . . . It's trifling. I know very well that this aversion is, for many of us, expressed in our indifference. But there is more. . . . In the end, the death of a pagan, savage or not, is less dramatic than the death of a bourgeois Christian.

We have fabricated for ourselves a little history that becomes more and more confining, in which life is hidden because death is inadmissible within it.

Annie: Yet it remains true, I believe, that we can very well have an open attitude toward our own death when we have understood the sense of life. It is the death of others that is terrible. Sometimes I break out into a cold sweat when I think that my daughter could die, will die.

Marie: Not me. I now believe that death is good and that it comes easily. Certainly, I don't like to think of the deaths of my children; that would be dreadful. But it would be dreadful for me, not for them.

Annie: Granted, the death of others is difficult to take. Earlier, when you told me how the death of others in the recovery room frightened you, I thought of the delivery of my child. I truly lived through that in a very intense manner. It was one of the most impressive moments of my life and I would like to live it again. Just afterward, I heard a woman in the next room who was delivering and I said to myself, "I wish it were over, I wish it were over." I couldn't stand it.

Marie: As I did; at that time I accepted my own death but refused to accept the deaths of others. Why? It's interesting.

I'm trying to remember. . . . It was when I heard others dying or in agony next to me that I panicked. The noises that they made were what I couldn't bear. Yet these noises are the same as those of lovemaking: these gasping breaths which quicken, stop, begin again, these shivers which come from the centers of ourselves. In hearing these noises, did I unconsciously link them to sexuality and to all the taboos that sexuality carts around with it?

Annie: I understand what you mean, that this touches the absolute depths of our mystery. When you make love, you don't hear these rattlings, you live them. It's true that I don't like to hear people who are making love.

Marie: It shouldn't be unbearable to us, just as the deaths of others shouldn't be unbearable. It's just another proof that we are completely out of touch.

Annie: It really is a taboo. Yes, but this taboo isn't only the result of social repression. I think that it is something deeper. There is the darkness, the absolute unknown.

Marie: The absolute unknown shouldn't frighten us. Moreover, nothing is absolutely unknown; in one way or another, we make up the absolute, we participate in it; that shouldn't scare us.

I don't know if you remember this, but at the end of one of the first editions of *Tristes tropiques,* there were some photos, certain ones picturing men and women of an Amazon tribe making love. . . . Do you remember? There was nothing indecent about it. They made love in the dust with complete liberty, without the slightest vice, and what is more, their faces showed happiness. In the background of these photos there were other members of the tribe who went about their business, who cooked, got ready to go hunting, children who played. It didn't bother anyone that there were two others who wanted to fuck leisurely in the sun. And it didn't bother the lovers that the others did housework or picked their teeth nearby.

Annie: You think so?

Marie: Yes. But it's clear that we now have bad lines of communication with sex and death, two things which shouldn't scare us or disturb us, and even less constrain us. We've lost contact with them.

Annie: Even so, something will always remain deep within us that cannot be resolved, a certain number of questions relative to existence, to the world: Where do we come from? Where are we going? What is death, life, sex? We're thrown into the middle of it, and it doesn't make sense and never will.

Marie: Because you're looking for a sense and a human sense into the bargain. What isn't human is frightening. We only think of existence in human terms.

Annie: You mean in terms of the individual.

Marie: No, human. In our civilizations, everything leads us back to the human, to the human cut off from dream and imagination. Some want to explain everything to us and then say to us, "It isn't worth it to argue, it's just like that, it's proven." And that which isn't proven is dangerous, bad, and consequently doesn't exist. Everything must have a logical sense. Everything has a beginning and an end because it's like that in the so-called reign of the modern human, and outside of that, there is nothing.

I remember a program which aired on television very late one evening. It was a program about six or seven scientists who are present-day successors of Einstein. They came from every corner of the world: Japan, the United States, the Soviet Union, Sweden . . . researchers, physicians, mathematicians. In the end, they all said the same thing: we find nothing when we follow the road of the so-called rational, logical path. I remember that one of them had, for a long time, studied the zones of the cosmos against which radio waves strike. He explained very clearly that, logically, when something is stopped we think that it has met with an obstacle, a hard element, a barrier, a wall. And, in his research, he tries to understand this wall in the cosmos, to find it. And then one day, while he was taking a stroll, he began to daydream, to ramble; his spirit was romping far from the idea of his wall, far from his calculations, and he suddenly thought, "Why a wall and not a hole?" And, in reality, that was it. The waves were falling into a hole, an empty space, in which they traveled the circumference and left through the other side.

Our conditioning is very pervasive. We have life, history, an idea more and more narrow which suffocates people, alienates them, terrorizes them. The zone in which we are safe is minuscule. The more logically you think, the more you prove scientifically, the more you limit the size of man. Men mangle humanity, amputate it. We have stumps everywhere, in dream, sex, death, and life.

And along with all of that, as if that weren't enough, in order to reduce humanity into mockery, those who direct us and who give us food for thought also want to recover everything around them. You pick up a pebble, you look at it, think of it and you say, "If a pebble has an existence, what a boring existence it must be, so slow, so static. . . ." Look at people with their animals; they explain that their animals are intelligent, they understand everything, they love, they are afraid, all like us. Exactly like us. They believe that it's reassuring to put everything into human terms; while, on the contrary, that which plunges them into anguish is to want to understand everything, to explain everything, to appropriate everything to themselves. Yet ownership is alienating, distracting. And humanity is only a part of the universe. Humanity doesn't save the universe from non-existence.

For us, for westerners, it's even worse. Not only do we reduce history to reasoning humanity, but even more so to Cartesian, Christian humanity. Look, today, at the history of neocolonization. It's monstrous. If you are not American or European, you are abnormal or you're an idiot. In any case, you're in the lower class.

Annie: I wonder if you're not always pugnacious. As if you had an idea of what death or well-adjusted sexuality should be. . . . According to you, we should be able to live very simply with the fact that two people are making love along side of us. You cite the examples of these photos, and you seem to say that it should be like that. But for these people whose sexual practices are so open, simple, without all of the perversion, blackness, shame, and guilt that enters into our conception of it, I'm entirely right to wonder if this isn't also a manner of reducing a fundamental anguish. I'm not sure that we can say, "Well, this is what it should be."

Marie: The weight of life also weighs on these people. But if this weight leads them to anguish, it will be a more true, clear anguish, tied directly to the universe. While for us, we have lost that type of communication.

Annie: That is to say that they have harmonious solutions which agree more with the universe. It rolls along better; things work better. While for us, we never cease getting caught on something. We don't have the capacity to exchange something with others, old people, children, the universe, the past, the future.

Marie: We're no longer in the round.

In these peoples, when one of them is struck by a delirious fit, he becomes the most important person in the tribe during the time that he has the delirium. It becomes the occasion for a ceremony, a holiday. Their delirium is taken as a bond. Yet you see what we, ourselves, do with people who have fits of delirium? We put them in prisons or in psychiatric hospitals. We are ashamed of them, we condemn them, hide them, we want to do away with them.

I know that I burst through open doors and that I state the most simple truths. But in the course of the innumerable conferences to which I am invited in the provinces and in Paris, most of them organized by women, I am seized each time by the alienation of women; they are, in general, not in touch with what is written or thought in France. They are on the fringes.

That is normal, for in this society, there is no place for them. There is only a place for femininity.

Now, I am a woman and I was mentally ill. I was, therefore, doubly rejected by this society, doubly murdered by it; and naturally I don't like it.

I'm not saying that only men are capable of fabricating such a foolish, harmful society; reasoning reason isn't their privilege. I think that women are capable of creating something equally foolish and equally poor, why not? But in the meantime, women haven't created this society and it is notoriously bad for them.

I would like to engage in combat because I like to fight. (I know how to fight with words, of course. I don't know how to fight physically.) But in France not one political party, right or left, really supports the woman's cause. Not one.

I attended a meeting organized by the Communist Party on the occasion of the release of a book which discussed women. Georges Marchais led the debate. He explained to us for a good fifteen minutes that the cause of all our ills was the capitalist system, and that once the capitalist system was abolished, there would be no more problems for women. Then he gave the floor to the assembly. I got up and asked him, "Don't you believe that once capitalism is abolished, there will still remain a capitalist system in boxer shorts called 'man'?" The entire audience, which was composed almost entirely of women, applauded and burst out laughing. One woman at the meeting got up and, red-faced with indignation, retorted, "None of that here. We members of the party are all equal. There isn't any difference." I pointed out to her that there weren't as many women as there were men on the organizing board of the party. Georges Marchais added water to her wine and admitted that they sometimes had trouble naming comrades to posts of responsibility because they were women. . . .

One of my best friends, a member of the party, to whom I told this story, told me: "The proportion of women members of the party's organizing board is equal to the proportion of the women who vote Communist." I asked her if the number of bearded men or nearsighted men on the board corresponded to the Communist electorate who are bearded or nearsighted. . . .

It's the same in the Socialist Party, it's even the same in the extreme left. As for the rest, let's not even talk about it; for them it's still the nineteenth century.

Yes, I'd like to fight; but not for the right to sweep conference halls or to arrange bouquets on banquet tables, or to assure child care for congressmen's children. I've done that all of my life and I've had enough of it.

I think, rather, that women must enter into politics; if not, they will never leave their own ghetto. There must be numerous women in the town councils. The affairs of cities, towns, and villages are their affairs. They are more concerned than men are about the streets, the apartments, the businesses, etc., because they and their children are the principal users of them. This is what politics is in the beginning: the organization of a city.

It would be good for women to discover how they are manipulated, even in their most private lives. They must realize that in the name of "their feminine nature" they are made to do anything. At the beginning of the century, when we needed workers in the factories, it was proven to women by A + B that bottle-feeding children was best and that if they were good wives and mothers, they would stop breast-feeding and go give a hand to their men in the factories. Today, as we are in a period of unemployment, a movement breaks out, as if by chance, in favor of breast-feeding. They discover that the bottle creates mental defectives, delinquents and crazies.

... "If you are good wives and mothers, you must return to the home quickly and don't leave it; that is the way nature wants it." When will that end? When their arms are needed again outside of the home.

I can bear witness—because I see thousands of women each year—that women don't know that their "nature" is what politics and the economy want it to be.

I began working on this book—which isn't one—with an unexpected ardor, fiery spirit, and happiness. It took me away from my usual books, which are long, solitary, and tormented navigations between staggering tempests of exaltation, dangerous lulls of doubt, and long periods of silence. Let's say that the lot of the writer is a sometimes happy and often menaced solitude.

It is impossible for a writer to translate a book that is being written, or even one already done, into words. Each book is a theater of our memory; and, in our memory, the role of the unconscious is much larger than that of the conscious. So we don't know how to talk about it (and that's why these so-called "literary" radio or television programs really aren't "literary").

I think that each reader creates a different book than that which the writer has written. And because the writer himself doesn't know exactly what he's written, we can say in the end that a book is a printed object made of bound, spindled paper, which one person has written and another browses. As to its contents, that depends on the desire of the person who browses through it.

This time, I wasn't alone. I could talk to Annie about the book. That was pleasant. Of course I was on the carpet; but, most often, it was she who directed our conversations.

At a certain point in time, we decided together to stop taping conversations. It was time to get started. I had to get to work. I had to rewrite, to sort the good from the bad in our jumble of words. Progressively, the pages were born and I sent them off to Annie in packages. She commented on them. For example, she said to me, "You haven't spoken enough about blood." I reflected on that. Maybe I would be able to develop and clarify certain passages in the chapter about blood, but for the moment, I had nothing more to say on that subject. I would have had to read studies, statistics on the state of women's gynecology, but they don't exist. At least the studies which do exist about this matter were done by men or with the spirit of men. No one doubts the regularity of men-struation. I do doubt it. Simply because I was able to deter-mine at which point the soul is tied to this blood. I know that this blood is not only a simple psychological manifestation, one of the ways in which our bodies are programmed. It is more than that. But I can't prove anything. And then, I have already spoken a great deal about blood in my last book. Why does Annie insist so much on this point? Maybe she'll say in the part of the text that she is drawing up.

Summer came. As I had every year, I left for Canada. She went to Greece, to stay with her husband's family. According to our plans, the better part of the book would be finished when I returned. We were not going to see each other for two months. . . .

I was about to write "two years" instead of "two months," for what happened next disrupted our plans so greatly. But I'm getting ahead of myself. . . .

We had decided to have a last and long interview of four days before leaving for vacation. It was to take place at Annie's house in Limousin, in the house that her grandparents had built on the outskirts of the village where they were both teachers.

For me, Limousin sounds like an old French folk song: *Paimpol et sa falaise, j'irai revoir ma Normandie, la Bourrée en Auvergne, Montagnes Pyrénées-é-é,* etc. It sounds like all the French folklore that they taught us at school and that seemed as far away to us children of northern Africa as the mystery of the Incas or as China and its Chinese hat. Ah! For us, the countryside was Djurdjura, Sahel, Chélif, the gorges of Chiffa, the Monkey River, or the Amazon's Basin. But that wasn't sung. And it wasn't taught, as for all other French children, except in a small chapter in the big history and geography book.

From the window of the train I saw the most "countrified" country pass by, a very French countryside, with woods, fields, rows of gladioli, rusty lattices, fences askew, fat chickens, sleeping cats, slender and sinewy rivers: a foreign land!

Fortunately, Annie was at the station with her young daughter and then, I had my typewriter.

In the end, I spent four days in Limousin that were happy, full of sun, grasses, friendship, and beautiful trees. Days full of the emotion caused by the manuscript of Annie's book, which I gluttonously read in the sun-speckled shadow of an apple tree or in the shade of the tall wood pile. Days full of the village holiday and its torchlight parade, which we followed because Annie's daughter carried a multicolored torch, at the head of the troop, with the other country children. Firecrackers exploded in the warm night, yet their racket didn't seem to overpower the music of the fanfare, which, Annie told me, enjoyed a distinguished reputation in the area. All of this was lit by Bengali torches.

Immediately following that memory is the memory of the airplane in the great sky of the Atlantic. Above: the marine blue of the cosmos, the bluish black of the galaxy. Below: the emeralds of icebergs mounted in the ocean, just before reaching the Americas.

Montreal! And its new airport, which disrupted my arrival. Usually, I was on vacation at Jean-Pierre's almost from the moment I stepped off the plane. This time, the trip lasted an hour longer: the time to get to know the new buildings, the new hallways, the new rooms, the new odors of this place which had been rigged out for the Olympic Games. I wasn't arriving in Canada; I was arriving in the antechamber of the Twenty-second Olympiad.

Finally, the house on Craig Street, gleaming in my honor, newly painted, decorated with Chinese kites. Flowers. And Jean-Pierre's laugh, his eyes which look me over, recognize me, look tenderly, question. Friends everywhere. A salmon on the table. A wonderful new table! "This table is wonderful, where did you find it?" "A friend made it especially for me." Glasses that we raise in a laughing toast. News which tumbles down like a summer rain, thick and necessary. Their news, mine; until the year's chasm that separated us has been filled; until late in the night, tired, satisfied, we feel that we have been together until this very day.

Next will come the sunny days devoted to work and warmth. All it will take is to clean out my cave, to find my rhythm. I'll work well here. I have always worked well here. Just the time it takes to get over the jet lag—I will need four or five days—and I'll continue with the book.

I couldn't imagine that there would be this swoon, this exhaustion, this rupture. Like an earthquake, which would have dislocated the very core of my being, fully and profoundly.

It was evening. Jean-Pierre was playing in *Garden Party,* a show which began at midnight. The theater was very close to the house, but in spite of that he had to leave an hour early to do his makeup, to dress and to make sure of the lights and the props.

I had hardly arrived, and that evening, I felt jet lag torturing me. I thought it would be better for me to stay at home and doze for an hour than to sleep standing at the theater. "I'll meet you later. I think I'm going to sleep a bit." "OK. I'll see you later."

I started reading and then felt that I wasn't going to fight against sleep that night. It was invading me, heavy, light, dark, clear, drowning the moment, stirring up my dreams. Useless to resist it. I'm going to bed. My bath; my bed. My book with my glasses to which I'm not yet accustomed, because they are a threshold of old age and that seems improbable to me, impossible, funny. Me, grow old? It makes me laugh. Every time I put my glasses on, I mimic a grandmother: agaga, agaga. It's a masquerade that I put on for myself alone. He who laughs last. . . .

It was warm that evening, that sticky heat of Montreal which at the slightest movement makes you sweat. It was the very first Sunday of the Olympic Games. The streets were full of big, gleaming cars which pulled their supple weight to the doorsteps of the Saint-Denis, the Berry, and the Craig, just before climbing the ascent which leads to Old Montreal. They resembled multicolored beetles with red and yellow eyes which lit the glistening spots of the street lamps.

The ardent, teeming city, in whose arteries ran the blood of celebrations, and me in my room lit by the pleasant light of a Chinese lantern, a ball of ivory-like paper, alone, at rest, nude, with my book and my glasses. I didn't read for long. Sleep took me before I had time to put out the light. Before sleep closed the doors on my dreams, I simply pulled the corner of a sheet over my body, relaxed by the cool bath I had just taken. I left for a night of vacation like a big white yacht crossing the waters of perfumed islands.

A bit later, something disturbed the deep sleeper I had become: a movement of the bed, a crag that I had to navigate appeared in the path of my delicious swim. I only took the time to think, while continuing my slow, flowing stroke, "Jean-Pierre has returned." And then, again, plunging even more calmly, more agreeably, into my warm wave populated by shells and seaweed, golden sands, and blue-tinged streams.

The bed moved again, several times. It moved so much that I now swam in a channel full of rocky reefs. I had to pay attention, I had to return to the surface of life. I must have smiled in waking because, just before I opened my eyes, I thought, "Jean-Pierre is drunk. He went drinking with the cast after the show as usual, but tonight he drank too much. He doesn't know what he's doing and he wants to lie down here, where I'm sleeping." I also thought that, perhaps, he wanted to make love and he was trying to wake me gently, nicely. I knew he'd see the mirth in my expression when I opened my eyes to him. . . .

. . . there, above me, very close to me, was the face of a man that I had never seen!

A young guy — about twenty-five, perhaps — with a patterned short-sleeved shirt, a blue background strewn with colored figures. He had curly hair parted on the side, reddish blond, and an expression above all, a horrible expression.

He was on all fours above me. Or, more precisely, when I saw him he was moving onto all fours. His right knee was already against my thigh, his right fist was against my shoulder, and his left side followed. He was certainly looking at me even before I opened my eyes, for the dangerous message that he bore was transmitted to me in that fraction of a second after I woke. I write that there was danger in his expression, but it was more than that: peril, menace, and total indifference, an absolute contempt. No fear of me, no curiosity either. I was an object, something which he could use without risk, a gadget that he knew how to handle.

Terror came immediately, as if a dam had burst, unleashing a devastating flood. Terror: is that the word I want? Fear. Horror. Panic. Repulsion. Is there a word to express the essential denial of rape? There isn't one. I was afraid of bombs during the war. In my childhood, I was afraid of the furious thrashings that my mother would give me using a belt and its buckle end. Sometimes I'm afraid of having an accident when I drive too fast. I've been afraid of death. I'm afraid of the compulsorily unjust sentence of judges, police, teachers, doctors, powerful people. Not one of these fears is comparable to the fear of rape, this murder which doesn't kill, this assassination which doesn't even hurt.

A sort of interior catapult released to raise my body. But the man was so close to me that, in order not to touch him, I had to brake hard against the movement which threw me forward. I braked so hard that only my head rose only scarcely, only a few centimeters. A face of shock flourished at the head of the infuriated magma that the tendons, muscles, and bone in my neck and shoulders had become. The unconscious effort which pushed me towards attack or defense, and the conscious effort which refused attack or defense. My face was now in the air, immobilized, and this conscious effort was forcing my eyes to look, drawing the corners of my lips toward the nape of my neck, petrifying the howl of distress in a huge block which couldn't pass through my open mouth.

The bridge which went from his eyes to mine and from my eyes to his was solid, and was the only pathway that life offered me at this moment. We saw everything. He knew my alarm, my surprise, my fear, the repelled attack, the resistance. I knew his determination, his indifference, the suppleness of his body which adjusted itself into position, no hesitation, no pause in his anticipatory movement.

Pieces of seconds passed, weighty as myths, the heaviness of human memories.

Vision of the white walls of my childhood bristling with shards of bottles, broken glasses, treacherous as fish hooks, cruel as arrows, violent as bullets. Insurmountable, primitive. With little painted flowers which remain caught in a gleaming broken piece (like the palm trees on the man's shirt) or letters still molded in the jagged neck of the bottle (like the carefully combed part in the man's hair).

Visions of the wounds that I would have if I passed that way. Lacerated flesh. Living meat. Gashes in the muscles to let out the budding blood. Digits amputated. Skin torn. Stomach burst. Eyes pierced. Arteries sectioned and the hemorrhage which would gush out everywhere in huge red jets, regular, warm, bespattering the fresh limestone.

The cry didn't burst out, not a gesture formed. I was there, paralyzed, entirely given up to wickedness and brutality. The obstacle was inhuman.

I let my head fall back and, at the same time, I mimicked a heart attack, a seizure. I began to choke, gurgle, gasp. Instinct made me do this, not reason. After that, when I saw myself doing it, I thought, "If he's a pervert, he'll rape me anyway. They rape anyone, children, old women, corpses. If he's simply a criminal, he won't want a corpse on his hands."

Through my eyelashes I saw him pause for a moment. Then, he moved quickly on top of me. He took my purse, which was on the corner of the bed, near my head, and then he quickly moved away, never taking his eyes off me. I thought of my glasses, "If he takes them I won't be able to write"; then I remembered that I was reading before I fell asleep and that, as a result, my glasses weren't in my purse. The rest of it I didn't care about. Let him take what he wants and leave.

I closed my eyes tightly and continued to make noise, working hard to portray a dying person, someone who is asphyxiated, an epileptic, anything terrible. For a long time I thought he was still in my room, at the foot of the bed. This presence sharpened the edges of my terror. My heart jumped in my chest, I felt my rib cage beat against the mattress with an unimaginable force. I tried to perfect my suffocations and spasms, but they became artificial, my imagination had run out. I was afraid that he'd sense the farce. So, I half opened my eyes. He wasn't there. The room was empty.

I thought that he was in the apartment, trying to steal more. I sadly thought of my typewriter, there was nothing more than that to steal in Jean-Pierre's place. Too bad. Let him steal the typewriter and leave. I could hear no noise. Nothing. What was he doing? And what if he returned! The silence was unbearable.

I called "Jean-Pierre!" knowing that he wasn't there. It was to give me courage, to bring me back to life. And then I decided to move. I got up, grabbed the bathrobe which was on the bed and fled out the kitchen, through the stairway, into the grass, barefoot, convinced that the man was still in the house. The pleasant sensation of the asphalt under the soles of my feet did me some good.

The street was full of revelers, drunks, people who were shouting. On this night of the Games, the five linked circles of the Olympiad seemed, absurdly, to be everywhere: lit up in neon above white poles, on the cotton T-shirts and paper hats of the night prowlers; they were a sign, a wink, of which I understood nothing. The cars, caught in congested traffic, inched along. I heard bits of drinking songs, laughs, American gibberish.

To get to the theater quickly, you must cut across a large, inclined parking lot which is usually full of gravel, broken bottles, rusty Coke cans. I wanted to avoid this poor short cut because of my bare feet and take the longest way around, via the sidewalks. At one point, the path was blocked. I had to wait for a car to pass, full of people at the point of lunacy, shouting and laughing. All the windows were open because of the heat, and I saw heads emerging from car doors wearing paper caps, arms gesticulating. One of the arms seized my bathrobe and the person belched out obscenities because I was barefoot: a dope addict, a junkie who had a bad trip and ran out into the street. He pulled. The nightmare continued. I shook him off brutally and decided to cross the parking lot. Too bad if I cut my feet. I preferred any wound to this sort of contact. I know that I was pale, disheveled, hunted, mad.

Until I found Jean-Pierre. Then I began to talk.

For the ten days that followed I believed that I was once again falling into mental illness. I was unable to remain alone, I was afraid of all strangers. I never left Jean-Pierre, and at night, while he slept, I stayed awake listening for noises, terrorized. Impossible to rest. We moved the bed. I wanted to buy bolts, make the place full of bolts. Everywhere.

My story had its effect on others for some time. Men said, "And you didn't do anything!" "Nothing." "You didn't even scream!" "Not even that." Women were moved, they asked for a lot of details, and they always finished by saying, "He didn't touch you?" "No, he didn't touch me." "Lucky for you." Then the story grew old. I felt that I was beginning to talk drivel, to talk only about that. I stopped talking about it So the images, the slivers of his expression, the bits of movement began to proliferate in the warm and well-scaled hot house of my mind.

I became a kind of dough that I would knead endlessly. Certain bits swelled, rose. I had to work them with all of my strength so that they didn't overrun everything, so that they didn't degenerate into madness. For example, movement on my left. The man supported himself on the mattress on the left side of my body. Since that incident, all that surprised me on the left side frightened me, all that which was on the left was suspect. I had to guard my left for my life.

I saw my face once again, tired, disgusted, my expression was absent. It was the expression that best hides the shameful disorder of the soul; the expression that best hides the enormous distance which empties out between the person who is losing the soul and others. To have found these gestures, attitudes and comportments again so quickly made me more afraid than my fear did. At every turn, I remembered a question asked by a psychiatrist during a debate: "Madame, do you think that you are in remission, or cured?" This man had been furious with me and with psychoanalysis since the beginning of the meeting; he wanted to hurt me. Never, until this moment, had I doubted my total cure. I saw myself as cured of my neurosis as one is cured of a cold. The man had asked his question with the seriousness and weight of a man of science. His tone made you understand that he knew what he was talking about, as opposed to me. I was surprised, and a tiny, minuscule doubt entered my soul. The audience felt it, there was a wavering, murmurs. Then, my joking retort, turning it back on him, reassured them: "I feel that I am totally cured. But if I'm wrong and if I fall again, I promise to consult you." The people laughed.

The story of the rapist/thief in Montreal had transformed the bit of doubt too quickly repressed into a frightening certainty. The remission was over.

However the anguish didn't return. I felt all of the symptoms. I trembled, I sweated, my heart beat quickly, but the undertow that took my reason with it, against which I was powerless, didn't return. My fear wasn't diffuse as it was during my illness. It was entirely localized in the story of the man on all fours on top of me.

I analyzed everything, husked off all of the outer layers. I put the tiniest detail through the sieve: the light, objects, clothes, movements, positions of the bodies, the time, place, and expressions. I fit each piece of this particular puzzle into the general puzzle of my life. The fear didn't go away. The necessity for bolts always obsessed me. I bought a big, gold one and put it up myself, quite well, on the lower part of the kitchen door which goes out into the hallway.

A woman's body doesn't have a bolt to close off the footpath which leads to her center, this part of her which belongs to her as much as her hands, eyes or hair, but which she doesn't know or control. There, where the heart, lungs, intestines, stomach, and the pouch where the child forms and grows all nestle. One only has to immobilize a woman, hold her legs apart, and even that isn't entirely necessary, and here she is, delivered to whoever wants to make use of the satin, humid, and dark path that penetrates into her greatest intimacy. An ant can rape her, or a worm, a finger, a speculum, and above all, a man's penis, which is made to go there like a hand in a glove.

We are made with holes in our bodies, and this hole is a terrible weakness. It makes us vulnerable. Whoever knows of the existence of this undefended passage knows, from that time on, that it can be used without risk. No muscle, door, sphincter, cartilage, or maze defends the access to the center of our bodies. To enter into this passage is tantamount to attaining what is beyond death: that is, in a daze to be the master of life. For the essential occurs in this place, at the base of the vagina, in the deepest part of the woman.

It is by this gap that we have been enslaved, and by it we have been defined. This definition and slavery are the rapes of our souls and our bodies, accepted since the beginning of time. Accepted because we cannot do otherwise. Because our territory has this area without a boundary where the enemy can enter; because our body is, naturally, undefendable.

And we haven't been taught to defend ourselves; on the contrary, we have been taught to be passive. This man on my bed was absolutely of medium weight. I didn't think that he was physically stronger than me. But how do I fight? How could I begin to fight in this vulnerable position in which I found myself, lying on my back, only just covered with the end of the sheet? What would be the most efficient grasp? His expression told me not to move, that he could hurt me if I moved. I believed him and I didn't move, I didn't say anything. I only felt once more a crushing sense of powerlessness and ignorance. I reacted atavistically: I remained passive and I looked for the response elsewhere, in lie and in farce.

We have fallen into the habit of submitting. We don't even know that we submit. Men have also forgotten that we submit. They call it our nature. We believe that it's our lot. To proclaim that this is absurd is to make positive proof of insanity. Nothing changes. What woman wouldn't think, going out alone at night, of the street that she'll travel in the darkness? What woman wouldn't calculate whether she is going to walk on the sidewalk or squarely in the middle of the street? What woman doesn't decide in advance on the attitude that she'll adopt if she sees a man or men appear in her path? And all of this in the midst of civilization, in our countries, which boast of their refinement today.

A jungle exists in our countries with animals who hunt and those who are hunted. The brutality of one group, the calculations of the other.

When someone tells me that sexual misery is the greatest of all miseries, that there is nothing lower, that it's the worst, I understand, I know that that's true. But this isn't a reason for women to continue to be passive; they don't have to enter into this demagogy; they don't have to continue to make this sacrifice. Because rape (all rapes, not only those of our bodies, but also those which we suffer in our daily lives) is above all a bad habit that men have developed: a woman is a sex object.

It was that which made me ill, which tormented my soul: repressed revolt, annulled refusal, ignored repulsion, belittled disgust, invaded territory, scorned integrity. All that which, in the end, makes men declare war. All that which makes women live in passivity and shame, while war rumbles formidably within us!

Rape is intolerable. Rape is a crime. Rape leads to insanity!

Annie: You should also talk about yourself when you aren't belligerent. We should understand how you could live through such great difficulties. Moreover, we should know how you lived, for example, at the level of your sexuality, something which was immediately successful.

Marie: Yes, in that sense I've had a fulfilling life without any problems.

Annie: That's important because that means that the blooming of a woman's sexuality mustn't be confused with the blooming of the body. That's why I don't like it when, in talking about a woman who has problems, someone says, "She's frigid." I think that's terrible. That would mean that from the moment a woman experiences orgasm, she has her reason for existence.

Marie: If there's a woman who can serve as proof of the contrary, it's me, because I've never had sexual problems and yet I dragged around enough problems to form a huge neurosis in which I almost lost my senses.

Annie: And you lived through all of your pregnancies and births quite happily?

Marie: Absolutely. The only comment to make on this is that I was only pregnant when I wanted to be. I had children during a very short period of five years. That's all. I never had an abortion. And what's more, I never did anything with contraceptives.

Annie: Do you have any idea about what determines the sexual success of women? Because, in the end, this poses as many problems as the lack of success. Why does it work in some cases and not in others? Me, for example, I've had a difficult time approaching sexuality. I've been vexed. How do you explain that?

Marie: If I could give an explanation, I'd make a lot of people happy. I don't know the first thing about it! Anyway, I don't think that this is tied to sex.

I think that it comes from the start, the beginning, the first time. I was lucky enough to find boys who loved me, who had patience, and who were gentle with me. They didn't pester me, nor did they rape me or force me in any way. They were respectful. When I think of the first boy with whom I made love, I realize that he was careful not to act until the moment I was ready to accept him.

Annie: In the end, what is the determining factor for you?

Marie: Respect.

Annie: This is the first relationship.

Marie: At the beginning nothing was done against my

will. On the contrary, everything was done with great attention to my desires. I'm grateful to the boy with whom I made love the first time. He didn't shock me, frighten me, hurt me, or make me feel dirty.

Annie: Your case is exceptional. That is, it's very rare to meet a woman who has had such a comfortable relationship with sexuality from the beginning. Men's approaches were, and still are, brutal. They are constraining approaches which seem like rape. For most women, isn't the first meeting with a man's sex an exhibitionistic spectacle? What aggression!

When I first began to make love, I was consenting. In a way I told myself that it was time to do it. But if the men with whom I made love had been truly attentive to me, they would have seen that I wasn't ready and they would have waited until I was.

Marie: That is how it happened for me. The boy knew that I was over twenty, that I was a virgin, had never even flirted. He knew that I wanted all of that but that there were a number of religious, familial, and moral taboos which kept me away from the slightest sexual life. At first, this absolute virginity seemed something heroic and pure to me. But as the years passed this virginity weighed more and more heavily upon me. I thought that it was nothing but a perversion of the soul, a worthless hypocrisy. The boy knew all of that; he also knew that I didn't love him any more than he loved me. He was in love with a married woman who was inaccessible. He admired me. We got along well. He was so patient! I remember very well that he kissed me for the first time in March and that I didn't go to bed with him until August. I think that at first he thought I was telling him stories. But when he realized that I really didn't know anything, well, then he took his role as initiator seriously. He felt a responsibility and played his role perfectly until the very end.

I made love for the first time in a neutral place, a hotel, far from my own town, far from my family, but in his town where he knew everything and everyone. After several days I went to his house. He felt that I was ready then to live in true intimacy, that I wouldn't be overwhelmed by his house, his friends, his habits, his genuine odor, his rhythm. It was done easily, happily.

Evidently, after that I wasn't afraid of sex, wasn't afraid of love. I can even say that at this time in my life, it was the only good thing in my life.

Annie: Don't tell me that you've always met up with men like that.

Marie: No, of course not. After that I sometimes (rarely) encountered what we call the "classic male," the "macho," the phallocrat, the one who thinks that a good fuck is always good for a woman. I've found this pretension laughable, grotesque, and I've never allowed myself to enter into this dance, to receive what certain people have the gall to call "a gift." Perhaps that's why rape is so repugnant to me, revolts me so. It is exactly the opposite of the act of love. To make love well is to give each other mutual pleasure. It isn't easy, in the beginning, to lead a woman to orgasm. The act of love is situated very far from the place that we give it in our societies. It has nothing to do with the shape of the body, with makeup, with age, etc. It is situated in a place of confidence and truth which is often difficult to find because the roads that lead there have been obscured.

We lead girls to believe that if they roll their hips right, if they have a pouting mouth and a sensuous glance, they will have a successful sex life. We think so. . . .

Annie: That is, we lead them to believe that sexual happiness is linked to the desire and the pleasure that they are going to arouse. In the end, they will have as much pleasure as they give.

Marie: This is still very obvious in France. What is popular today with certain American young people is that they don't make love for aesthetic reasons or so-called sexual reasons. They make love because they get along well; they call it "vibrations." I find the word a bit too descriptive, but it expresses what they want to say fairly well. It is because of this that you can see couples there that would be unthinkable in France. Women who are truly dowdy (to French men), with an overbite, obese or skeletal, with messy hair, and a man who is magnificent. Or, you see exactly the opposite: a woman who is splendid with a terrible-looking guy. Those that I knew had happy homes with wonderful children.

In France, things haven't changed a bit. I know what I'm talking about because I have two daughters, aged eighteen and twenty. One has always been ravishing according to the canons of modern beauty. And the other reached the end of adolescence a bit plump. I can tell you that the behavior of the boys that they met was exactly the same as that of the boys in my childhood. The daughter who was five pounds overweight had disappointments that the other one didn't have.

Annie: It's the same way with my students. I have co-ed classes and I see very clearly how boys will gather around a girl; it's always the prettiest girl. She not only has to be pretty, she also has to be someone who is vivacious and original.

Marie: People speak without knowing. They talk about today's corrupt youth. As for me, I believe that young people today have sexual problems which are even more significant than those of my day.

Annie: For women, there is a tyranny of beauty. They know that if they want access to sexuality, as long as they want it, they have to pay attention to beauty, they must make themselves as beautiful as possible. It's an amazing compromise, because they can feel that this attention to beauty is a humiliation. . . . The relationship to a body that must be beautiful isn't easy!

Marie: It's terrible, it torments women constantly. It warps everything.

Annie: Sometimes, during my adolescence, I used to

think, "At least I'm not ugly." I was right to think that. It isn't that I flaunted my beauty or my nonugliness. But if I had been ugly, how many doors I would have found closed! If I had been ugly, I would have had a different life, another world would have been given to me.

Marie: Ugly women live in a difficult world. I lived as if I were ugly. And when I was sick, I realized that if I had had a different physique, my sickness would have been taken more seriously. I had a look that didn't go with a mental illness. I have always been large, tall, athletic. The doctors that I went to see because of my periods of anguish told me, "But you're the picture of health. Here, go take such and such a pill, such and such a capsule, and it will go away in a flash." It didn't go away, and when I went to see them again, they began to take me for a hypochondriac, a woman who was playing games with them; because, with a physique such as mine, so sound, I couldn't really be "disturbed." They talked with my husband in the hallway, man to man. They must have tried to make him say that I had a lover or that he had a mistress. . . . That's how Jean-Pierre got into the habit of telling me, "But nothing is wrong with you, absolutely nothing. If you feel like that, it's because you don't participate in enough sports. You don't get out enough." I often thought, "Oh, if only I could break both of my legs!" There was an entire period where I thought that I would take an ax and cut off one of my legs. That way, they'd see that something was the matter.

It is truly difficult not to have the currently accepted physique. In France, people haven't yet begun to step out of physical stereotypes. The young people know something about that: from the moment that you have long hair, you become a revolutionary. . . . Unfortunately, that's not true!

Annie: You realize the number of women that still believe that if they were beautiful, they would be happy. Everything is still there to persuade them of this.

Marie: Our streets, walls, and heads are full of these model women.

Annie: They surround this woman who can't blossom except by becoming a sexual object.

Marie: But why do men, who never stop failing utterly with "beauties," continue to want to fabricate them and consume them? Why are they so dumb? What have we put into even their heads? They now know that happiness, sexual harmony, the harmony of a couple, is not tied to appearance. What's wrong with them that they still want it?

Annie: I think that it's because they are still attached to a representation of sexuality in which a beautiful woman is an object, precious to possess in the face of others. "I had that one, not you." I don't understand why a woman with beautiful almond eyes and well-placed breasts will satisfy a man more than another woman could. It is evident that it doesn't happen there. . . .

Marie: Yes, but they know it too.

Annie: That doesn't prevent them from always searching for the companionship of beautiful women.

Marie: That's terrible! And above all, it is in our country that this happens. Everywhere, in every class, whatever you do. If you don't have the slightest physical attractiveness and you are a woman. . . .

Annie: . . . you're not lucky.

Marie: Take a woman like Margaret Mead, who is ugliness itself. In her own country she was always listened to, always taken seriously. Can you imagine such a homely woman in France, publishing things of the sort that she publishes? No one would listen to her, or it would stay behind the scenes.

Annie: She would be, after all, too homely.

Marie: Do you know a truly unattractive woman who has succeeded in making her voice heard in France? I, myself, don't know any. All the women who have been able to express themselves have something seductive about them. They are, at least, made up, with carefully done hair. We can't imagine that these inspired American women who look as if they came right out of a trash can could be listened to a priori.

But be careful, because she mustn't be too pretty. That means she's not serious. If a woman is too pretty, she must make herself more unattractive in order to be taken seriously. . . . It's pure simplicity. . . . What would Mr. Sanguinetti say if he had to put on lipstick and straighten his hair in order to show his ugly face on TV? And Sartre, should he have to put on false eyelashes? And Poulidor, if he had to hide his legs now that he's growing old. As for Giscard, he absolutely couldn't avoid wearing a wig. . . . Just imagine that! It would be insulting to ask them to fix up their ugliness or their faults. It's unthinkable. Yet what more do these men have than Arlette Laguiller, Marguerite Yourcenar, Kiki Caron, or Indira Gandhi? Nothing. Absolutely nothing. Can you imagine Golda Meir as prime minister here? Impossible.

It's a universal phenomenon, but in France it is par ticularly evolved. I remember that I was completely scandalized at first when I began to live in North America to see women go out shopping with hair curlers on their heads, in walking shorts that didn't hide their varicose veins, and wearing simple bras buried under cushions of fat. The American population is generally unattractive, often obese, pot-bellied. These women had dressed, they felt clean and at ease. It didn't bother them at all to show themselves in this garb. A French woman, never. Even if she went out to cross the street, she wouldn't dare be seen like that. I looked at these American women and I said to myself, "That's not right. They could have at least taken the curlers out of their hair."

Annie: How do you explain that?

Marie: These are women who have lived a difficult life. Because even the beginning of America's existence was difficult. They succeeded, such as they were, naked, coarse, poor, harsh, with their men, in making this enormous country. They have proven that they don't need aesthetics to succeed. Today, aesthetics are something extra for them. They deck themselves out to go to parties. If you saw the hats they put on their heads—unbelievable: entire gardens, aviaries, tempests of tulle. And lamé dresses and jeweled shoes. Their beauty is an exterior sign of their wealth, it means that their husband is financially successful.

Annie: Whereas in our country beauty has another meaning.

Marie: It's a trap for cretins.

Annie: Yes. I remember a very simple and modest woman whom I liked very much when I was little. She said to me, "Oh my, my! You have the eyes to make a man's fly buttons jump off!" That really made an impression on me because I wasn't certain that I understood. When I got older, I understood: it was as if beauty was, for us, directly linked to sexual solicitation.

Marie: I tell you, it's a veritable trap. Because it is beauty which determines the Frenchman's choice where women are concerned. But this beauty is the veil which covers the merchandise. Underneath beauty, the man must have not only a good lover, but also a good cook, a thrifty woman, a good mother, wife, nurse, seamstress, washerwoman, etc.

We girls know these demands very well. They have been impressed on us since birth in all social classes. Rothschild's wife keeps Rothschild's house. True, she does it with maids, footmen, and all the rest of it. True, she is a "maid de luxe" with diamonds, furs, and yachts. But to define her, you need only say, "She is Rothschild's wife," just as we say, "That's the plumber's wife," or "That's the store manager's wife." That is, what defines Rothschild's wife is to be the wife of this gentleman.

All right, let's close the parentheses around this rich

woman. This example served only to say that all women know that beneath their beauty, they must have essential and important housekeeping qualities. And when they don't feel very much like washerwomen or menders or nannies, they add a layer of red or black or blue, they mold their skirts more carefully to their bottoms and their sweaters more carefully to their breasts. They do that even when they don't feel truly sexy. It's too much! I don't know how many women I've met who are dressed up like princesses, made up like actresses, with the allure of stars and voices which could excite cadavers, who have never or almost never experienced orgasm in their lives, who don't even like to make love.

Yes, coquetry is a powerful trap which makes fools of men, but makes fools of us women as well.

At least for the Americans it's clear: their coquetry says that they have enough money to buy the trophy, the tool box, the equipment for the beautiful woman.

Annie: It's interesting because these are two forms of alienation. But we can't say that one of these forms is better than the other. The American woman parades the social status of her husband. The French woman, on the other hand, parades her husband's qualities as a lover.

Marie: Of course. And it's also illusory. All Americans aren't rich and all Frenchmen don't make love well. . . . The only sense in these masquerades is that they are expressions of Puritanism and Catholicism, the two religions that are the basis of our respective capitalisms. Two women, two religions, two variations on a theme: possession. For women in these societies, the job is to possess a man. And they can spare no expense, because a man is expensive.

And what if we talk about desire, pleasure, or the game. Just how far can we go on these streets? Because these are the domain of men.

Annie: Orgasm?

Marie: The paths that lead to orgasm: pleasure, de-

sire, the game. Have we ever spoken about it in the feminine?
Perhaps there is no feminine desire. Perhaps the feminine
condition engenders a desire that is completely affected. Are
we capable of a desire, a pleasure, a game that is different
from that of men? When we play the game or show desire or
have orgasms, are we simply doing this to trap a man or to
mimic him? In all of this is there something which is really
our very own? That has never been expressed. Are women's
seductive behaviors this way because it is our nature to play
the game this way, or rather are they this way because men
have wanted us to play like that to please them?

    Annie: I think that women have spoken of their plea-
sure and their desire, but always within the permitted limits.
I think of Colette, who spoke in an extraordinary manner
about her pleasure and her desire, but always within the
borders of the admissible. She said it in a foreign, astonishing
manner; but at the same time, it was always what was permis-
sible to say.

    Marie: My first book was the dawn of my birth, my
cure. I ventured into these first blank pages the way a lost
woman in the desert would find a sign of water: with an
unspeakable joy as well as with an extreme uncertainty and
anxiety. What if there was no water! What if I had been
mistaken in beginning to write? This first book was one of the
most important events in my life, perhaps the most important.
And, too, I was aware that my act of primary importance was,
at a second level, also done to recover Jean-Pierre, from
whom my illness had separated me. I told a love story about a
man who wasn't him and, on top of it all, I dedicated the book
to him. And it worked.

    What perversity there is in all of that. Am I perverse?
Or is perversity a part of the game that men demand of us?

    The phrase, "As happy as a fish in water" is accurate.
For when I go to Karl's house, I am as happy as I was during

that blessed time when I was swimming six hours a day. I know the road to his house by heart. It carries me. There are underwater roads that I know by heart. I float. . . .

Paris nights swim around me. They swim slowly through the streets bordered by vacant lots: a light, shadow, another light, and again shadow; it is a printed cloth, a hand which comes to the surface from time to time, striking and satisfying.

I am coming, Karl, I am coming! Oh my sea, my great sea.

They swim madly through the crossroads: electric signs, store windows, streetlights, red, yellow, and green lights. These are the arms and legs of a vigorously churning, thrashing crawl.

I am almost there, Karl, I am coming! Oh my blue, warm, gentle sea.

Coming to your house, I do the powerful and classic breast stroke through the avenues, the heavy butterfly through the boulevards.

It is done, Carlito, I am at your door! Oh my liquid plain, my beloved, my trembling, flowing daughter, how beautiful you are!

Slam the car door in the true lofty night which encroaches upon the houses. Cross a courtyard, and another, and finally begin the urgent climb. The eleven flights turn around the narrow incline. Turn, turn, more and more slowly, to the top, to the closed, welcoming door. I have trouble breathing. My lungs are smarting. If I let myself, I would pant like an animal.

I never say a word to Karl when he opens the door for me. Only a rattle leaves my mouth, the noise of a defective machine. I pass in front of him. He says, "Hello, you, how's it going?"

I don't reply, but I grunt a little to say that everything is fine, thank you. I enter the studio, flop down onto the bed and, with my head in the pillow, find the rhythm of my breathing once more. Karl sits near me, caressing my back gently, as he should.

"You see how your Karl lives so high? Do you know how many steps it takes to reach his flat?"

"I don't want to know. If you tell me, I'll never come back."

"I'm going to tell you and you'll come anyway. There are two hundred and seventy-eight."

"Oh my my my my!"

"Will you come anyway?"

"Yes."

"Really, I believe that you love this poor Karl."

"Perhaps. I hope not."

"Why?"

"Because love, for me, has always been unhappy, and I've had it with being unhappy."

"You will be unhappy if you want to be. Unhappiness comes when you wait for it."

I let him talk. I know everything that Karl says. Things like, "The pitcher that often goes to the well gets broken in the end." Or, "Meddle and smart for it." Or, "A rolling stone gathers no moss." He lives them, I don't; he's a peasant. I know all of that like I know there are twenty-four hours in a day and three hundred and sixty-five days in a year. It has only a theoretical sense for me. For him it has a practical sense, it is what regulates his life.

I let him calm my breathlessness, I let his hand fully open my back to the night, the lights, the sea. . . .

. . . there are underwater streets that I know by heart.

Aoued speaks. I listen to him. The heat and the sunshine fall in a rectangular shape through the rectangular opening of the sulfate warehouse. Aoued and I are seated on two blue, green, turquoise sacks in the shade, on the far side of the longest side of the cube of light, as if we were sitting at the edge of an incandescent river. Sheltered from harm, from what makes life impossible at three in the afternoon: the furnace of the sky which makes everything pale. The earth is gray, the sky is white, the trees are beige. He says, "Pierre is kind."

"Yes."

"Last year's workers will be accepted first," he said.

"Yes."

"That's good. Because if last year's workers come to work during grape gathering this season, that's because they like to work here."

"Yes."

"That's because Pierre's mother is kind and everyone knows her."

"Yes. . . . Say, Aoued, why don't you knit your socks anymore?"

"Maria, I never knit during grape gathering. There's too much work."

He plucks the largest feathers from the rumps of geese, he strips them nearly to the end and makes needles with which he knits rough spun wool made by his mother. Slowly, he brings forth socks that are stiff as hoses and which smell of lanolin. Knit one, purl one. Aoued taught me how to knit. I have normal needles that are red; Aoued admires them. They work as well as goose feathers, with their white tuft at the end. They are peaceful arrows.

". . . turn over, Maria."

Karl unbuttons the buttons of my coat one by one, the clips, the clasps, the closings. Free from my clothing, all bonds. Let the cables loose!

. . . how far away you are, my ripe clusters of grape gathering season, blue with sulfate and blood, golden with the sun. Containers full of them arrive at the cellar. Youssef tramples them with his feet. Yellow and mauve clusters. It gives him red stockings which come right up to his pants, rolled above the knee. He calls me to come and dance with him in the grape juice.

"Ma-ri-a."

. . . Ma-ri-a.

"Yes. Yes."

Karl's hand stops at the hollow of the stomach, where the skin is very smooth and supple.

. . . the flies play in the blinding cube of light. They buzz.

". . . I like your breasts."

"You're crazy. They're awful, they're sagging."

"I like your breasts; they're beautiful, they're heavy, they're not sagging."

This calm, large, gentle hand. This hard, long leg, perfect, which rests folded upon my stomach.

. . . they buzz, buzz. Not all in the same tone. They buzz when they fly: quick, short flights. As soon as they land, they begin their swift trick: their legs clean their wings, then their heads, and then they begin again. Numbers of little legs, flattened and agile. You might say that they were putting on and taking off an invisible sweater. Never ending, never ending. It's hot. Aoued speaks at times.

"The Parisian loves you."

"He's nice. . . . Why do you call him 'the Parisian'?"

"Because his father was in the war. He went to Paris."

The Parisian has white skin and green eyes. He has blond hair. He wears a large hat with tufts of red and orange and bits of leather sewn into the straw.

It is the time that one takes an afternoon nap. It smells of sulfate and dust. . . .

. . . Karl's hair is soft. His nape is soft. His shoulders are soft. His belly is soft. His inner thighs are soft, too. All of this softness calms me, penetrates me, makes me happy. I stretch, ripple, expand.

. . . the small waves, bordered with ermine, come

toward me and then draw away, taking a bit of the sand beneath my feet. The sea is a coquette. At midday, the sea is a coquette; but she will go to sleep in the end. The sea at four in the afternoon is direct, it wants to polish my skin, to glaze it. It wants to enter all of me. I must fight it with my legs, my loins, my arms. It slips between my fingers, onto my lips, onto my eyelids. It is nervous and exciting.

I accept its game: I plunge into its wave, limbs spread wide and released, breast forward.

. . . Karl is so powerful, there above me, the buttresses of his extended arms.

The seaweed moves with the rhythm of the water, at a slower pace. Its movement is supple and long, certain and effective; the movement doesn't end. It is natural.

"Karl. . . . "

He bends his arms a bit to bring his face nearer to mine. He is absorbed by the possession of this prize, so happy to be taken. His expression is troubled. He wants to know why I called him from the far reach of my beloved wave: Karl!

"Ja."

"Ich liebe dich."

He lowers his head to the hollow of my shoulder. His lips glide over my neck. He gives me his forehead with an infinite gentleness, even more moving because of the hard, combative form that the rest of his body expresses. He murmurs very deeply, very slowly, "Ma-ri-a . . . I . . . love you."

The water rushes against the rocks, crackling, leaping. In its flux it brings the smell of pines and fig trees that it swaps for the odor of seaweed and seashells in its reflux. It is a necessary mixture.

Aoued says, "The Parisian will dance again at the grape gathering festival this year."

When the Parisian dances, he lets himself be taken by the rhythm until he becomes the rhythm itself and, at this moment, collapses powerless, unconscious, asleep in the contemplation of the mystery which he discovered and in which he participated for one brief moment. His white body is stretched along the red earth to which he belongs.

Annie: Can you tell me what it means to you to write when you are in love?

Marie: For a love affair not to prevent me from writing, it must enter into my definition of the norm, it must leave me free, it mustn't change me.

Annie: And what would this norm be?

Marie: It would be, purely and simply, the disappearance of the man as he lives today; in other words, of that man who makes me be a woman as she is supposed to be. That is, the disappearance of virility and femininity. If I want to enter into the game of femininity, I must compose a character, I must abandon myself to find this woman. Thus, I am not free, and therefore I cannot write. I cannot support the banal, normal life of a couple. That doesn't prevent me from thinking that two free beings can form a couple.

Annie: So, you would like a couple that isn't a couple.

Marie: The couple is the subject of my next novel, and it's a subject for which I have a passion. I do not believe in the Mr./Mrs. couple, or the man/woman, or the male/female, as they are understood in our society. Yet I believe in a couple, only differently.

Annie: I note the fact that you entangle yourself in the regular and the irregular, the normal and abnormal. You say, "I want this to become normal." And when you say that something is normal, it is completely abnormal. There must be a couple, a man and a woman; but there mustn't be a couple. There shouldn't be "man" and "woman."

Marie: Exactly that. We return to the vague, which satisfies me and outside of which I don't believe that we can have a true existence.

All of these words, "couple," "normal," "abnormal,"

need to be redefined, rethought. We must enrich them, enlarge them, not let them harden in the dead thought that is ours at the moment.

If you say to me that a man and a woman form a couple only if they live with each other every day, have material problems together, have children together, well, I don't agree with you. I think that a man and a woman can form a couple outside of the day to day, outside of children, material obligations, and money.

Annie: The word "couple" bothers me. It would be good to live as you say, but I would no longer use the word "couple" to describe that life.

Marie: Yet I find that this is the most fitting word. The problem is that I don't live like you do. You, you live every day with your husband, your children, in your house. Me, I have been married for twenty-three years to a man who lives six thousand kilometers away, with whom I have had three children; and that doesn't prevent us from forming a couple, and even a very united couple. Moreover, it doesn't prevent me from forming couples elsewhere, less important, with things and people, even with other men. I think that a true couple can only exist in freedom. Each union must be a choice; if not, it isn't a union. As for sacred unions or unions in sacrifice, that is hypocrisy. It is sordid, the exact opposite of the couple.

Annie: In you, there is a perpetual oscillation between a subversion of the norm and a desire for order. But this vagueness and this freedom that you urge isn't livable and it isn't durable.

Marie: You can imagine that I don't agree with you, because I have been living that way for twenty-five years, and the longer it goes on, the better it is. I am speaking of the couple that I form with Jean-Pierre.

But I know that to question the couple is an extremely subversive action. To question the couple is not only to question the life of men and women, it is to question the family as well, and it is above all to question society. To wish to change the couple is to wish for revolution.

In France, when a person isn't a capitalist, he's a communist. As if there were no other solution! I assure you that when I think of the couple that I form with Jean-Pierre, solid and dynamic, I feel that a revolution exists, different from the kind to which we usually relate. We work, we have raised three children, and are therefore five in number; we have many friends, we like bread and butter, cheese and wine, and love. Not one of the five of us has been imprisoned, or gone crazy, or gone bankrupt. Not one of us has died of hunger or cold. We have decent clothes, we live in bright places, and we are not being eaten by vermin. And yet we live entirely outside of the traditional couple and family.

Annie: Theoretically that is possible, nothing stands in the way of it.

Marie: Why do you only say "theoretically," when I live it every day? For twenty-three years I have been married to a man I have known for twenty-six years, as a matter of fact. And I can assure you that we form a couple, a true couple, even though we are separated by an ocean, though we only see each other for a few months each year, and though we separately form appended couples with other ideas, objects, and people. But these appended couples have never, for a moment, taken precedence over the central couple that we form, he and I. I can even say that our couple is nourished and enriched by the appended couples that are formed outside of it. There is always water to turn the grindstone.

For me, the best definition of a couple is given in physics: two opposing forces which intersect at a fixed vector. What happens when one of the forces is more powerful than the other? What happens when the forces are equal? When the forces, instead of being opposite, go in the same direction, there is no longer a couple. When one of the forces disappears, there is no longer a couple either.

At the beginning of any couple there are always two opposing forces or, if you want, different forces. How can the Mr./Mrs. couple last? That is the problem. Because this Mr./Mrs. couple produces a family and our societies are constructed upon the family. That is serious.

So, how do we make the couple last? The forces must remain different and of equal power. We have been given certain things to make it last: children, love, money, common possessions. All of that is worthless. What I mean is that not one of these elements, in and of itself, makes a couple last. So, what makes it last? The only effective thing is the desire of the two forces to make it last. How to maintain this desire? In the majority of couples which surround me, this desire is only maintained by habit, flirtation, jealousy, selfishness, or the inclination of one of the two forces to definitively conquer the other. Not one of these solutions pleases me; I can even say that I absolutely reject them. And yet our couple has lasted for over twenty-five years.

We set off on our journey just like everyone else, and I believe that our boat would have foundered very quickly or would have become bogged down in the bay of mortal boredom if I hadn't had a great horror of divorce (because I lived through my parents' divorce very badly), and if I hadn't had, on the contrary, a fierce will to form a family similar to that which I had lacked and which I had never stopped imagining; a warm family, lively, inventive, gluttonous, welcoming.

Once the children were born, the boat all but disappeared, lost in the sea of agony with all hands on deck, lost in the sea of my illness. Jean-Pierre did what the captain of the ship must never do (for he was the captain; the thought never occurred to us that it could be otherwise): he left. He left me alone with the children. Enough to send you sobbing into the cabins. So, I stayed, crazy captain, to stop up a boat that was taking on water everywhere. But, nevertheless, I was captain. And I knew that, from shore, Jean-Pierre was watching my

every move. If the boat had sunk, he would have let it sink. But
the vessel survived and when Jean-Pierre returned on board,
we were two captains of equal competence.

The presence of their father on the shore, either seen
or unseen, always reassured the children. As far as my frenzied navigation, they didn't know that it was frenzied. They
thought that that was the way navigation was done. Now that
they are adults, they say that they never felt as if they were in
distress and that there were even very funny moments . . . and
others when they felt I was weary. . . .

What we ourselves understood was that in a couple,
one force must not prevent the other from existing in the
name of sacrosanct principles of the couple which fit it as well
as an apron fits a cow. Principles such as: the man commands;
the woman raises the children; the man needs certain freedoms to balance the exhausting work which he does in order
to feed everyone; the woman doesn't need freedoms because,
by nature, she only needs one man and because, in addition,
she is completely fulfilled by her children; the woman takes
care of the housework because, by nature, she is apt at this,
whereas the man isn't at all apt in doing housework; nature is
sound and it mustn't be contradicted. . . . We committed the
sacrilege of contradicting it, and you might even say we are
lucky to have done it.

I believe that the fuel or the wind which moves this
boat representing the Mr./Mrs. or the Mrs./Mr. couple is all
the couples that the Mr. or Mrs. form outside of the boat and
that they bring on board. The cargo of this boat/couple, its
richness, is all of the experiences the couple had individually
which are afterward shared.

Would you like to tell me if the woman who will not
tolerate her husband dropping an ash on the carpet is married to her husband or to her carpet? Who are the true
children of the woman who will not tolerate disorder? Her
furniture, her linen, her objects, or the little human beings

that she has brought into this world? What would be interesting would be if she were to first admit the principal importance of her accessories, and then try to understand what her carpet, her furniture, her dishes really mean to her deep down. If she took this step, she would discover a woman whom she has never met: herself. A woman with her own desires, tastes, impulses, and creativity, her own faults and her own qualities, not the faults and qualities of women in general. It is explosive!

It often happens that during her "little" household tasks, a woman catches sight of a door to her self. What she feels, when she tries to open that door, is so dizzying that, more often than not, she prefers to close it. My grandmother, who occupied a good part of each day with needlework, often said, "Ah, if our knitting could talk! . . ."

Women are imprisoned, silenced within their knitting, vacuums, sauces, laundry, canaries, bouquets, ironing, and mending . . . all secondary things.

I don't find them secondary, myself. I want for women to open them up, to peel off their husks, to talk about the wisdom that they have found in these tasks, as well as the science, the pleasure, the drama, the playfulness within them.

But, at this rate, what becomes of the couple? It bursts. Unless both of the forces of the couple yoke themselves to this type of work. Each couple has its own little ways. One thing is certain: if a couple emerges from this work, it will be a veritable couple, but will not be an orthodox couple as we understand the couple in our societies. And it will not create a traditional family. They will be a true couple, but a subversive, revolutionary couple.

All the more revolutionary because men will have to find out for themselves what ties them to their cars, to their mistresses, to their freemasonry, to war.

That would create a great hodgepodge! Many people urge this, but abandon it before they have even started and

content themselves with establishing a household like everyone else's. That is, it becomes a first class burial which lasts
thirty, forty, or fifty years!

Still, I think that the traditional couple is living
through its final death pangs, for women are beginning to
understand that they don't only exist as "women" but also
simply as human beings, and human beings who have vol-
umes to say.

For those who are against this evolution, which will
be a revolution in reality, I only see one measure to take to
prevent it: henceforth, prevent women from learning to read
and write; in any way you can, keep them distanced from
words. Leave them with only the language of the household
to express themselves, give them the language of cooking and
cleaning. And again . . . it's too late. They will find once more
the way to exist, thanks to cooking, cutting, fermentation,
birth, blood, guts, rot, dirt, water, air, meat, fish, egg, fever,
vomit, song. And everything will start anew. . . .

Annie: What you are saying is very clear, Marie, and I
understand it; but perhaps it is the use of the word "couple"
which makes what you say seem awkward, because you are
very disrespectful of its traditional sense.

Marie: I want to be.

Annie: When you speak of this possible couple, would
that mean that you could form a number of "couples" in a
single night?

Marie: Listen to you! Only put the word "night" into
that sentence and you imagine male/female couples madly
fornicating. We can form couples with anything, including a
lover, in order to use a word which goes with the word "night."

Annie: But all the same, you think that it is better to
form a couple with a lover than it is to form a couple with a
canary.

Marie: No, not at all. I don't think that at all. A lover, a
canary, a sauce, a piece of knitting, a bit of embroidery, it's all

the same. All of it is a desire to express oneself, to exist. Certainly, a sauce is seen as morally better than a lover; but basically it's all the same. There was an entire period of my life, when I was eighteen and twenty, that I adored embroidery. Afterward I had lovers, and I noticed that I turned to my lovers just as I had turned to my embroidery. I turn to my pages just as I turn to my lovers, aside from the fact that they satisfy me more and are more durable.

Annie: What you say is true. I have often heard women's words and reflections concerning erotic life which were much less clearly expressed than your ideas were, but which let it be known that women have known, and known for a long time, that erotic relationships are not exclusive of other relationships.

Marie: They know it, and I assure you that men don't want to know that they know it. Their virility is endangered by this idea. And God knows that their virility hampers them as much as our femininity hampers us. Only femininity is a prison while virility is a throne. It's easier to want to rid yourself of penal servitude than it is to want to rid yourself of a throne, even if that throne holds a chamber pot!

Annie: A woman's freedom is a terrible menace to a man. He needs the bond that attaches the woman to him to be very tight, so tight it hurts. A man admitted to me that I once said something terrible to him; I said, "You have never made me suffer."

Marie: I have a similar story. At the beginning of our life together, Jean-Pierre asked me why I married him and I replied, after having thought carefully, "Because you don't bother me." And today, after so many years, each time there is a conflict between us, he will toss out, ". . . besides, one day you said that I don't bother you. Which means that I don't exist, that you don't give a damn about me."

Annie: Yes, that's it. . . . We could ask ourselves if sadistic practices aren't a desperate wish to possess: "I can't

possess something like love. But there might be a substitu-
tion, and the moment that she suffers, she will belong to me."

Even in men who are aware of a number of things,
there is still such an impact of the virile ideology that it is in
this way that the ideology expresses itself; they can't get away
from it.

Marie: Note that women also make men suffer. But a
woman who makes a man suffer is a slut, whereas a man who
makes a woman suffer is a man.

To come back to the traditional couple, it seems to me
that the best example of its catastrophic effects is a program
that took place on the radio.

The producers of this program had a couple come into
the studio. They then separated them and began by asking first
the woman, for example, a series of three questions about the
possible behavior of her husband in a given situation. The
questions were of the sort: "Your husband is approached by a
woman of loose moral standards. Do you think that your
husband would continue on his way after having separated
from the woman, or that he would stop and talk with her before
continuing, or that he would follow her to a hotel. . . . ?" "These
are embarrassing questions," a taxi driver who was listening
intently while driving once said to me. The woman must give
a response which will stand as proof that she knows her
husband well. She must say, "My husband would react in the
first manner, or in the second manner, etc." Then they bring in
the husband, ask him the same questions, and he must say, "I
would do this or that." Then they do the same thing in reverse,
that is they make the woman leave and ask the husband
questions about his wife's behavior. Finally, if they have responded in the same way to the series of questions—all created
on the same vicious pattern that I have given—they will be
publicly declared a truly good couple and they will earn a
thousand, or two thousand, or five thousand francs, I don't
remember exactly how much.

How can such a game exist? For if the couple is a true couple that comes to the show to win the money that they need, the man and the woman have only to agree in advance that they will take the second response to the first series of questions and the first response to the second series, etc. Even if it entails passing themselves off as vicious or dishonest people. Which could be, since they themselves know that it isn't true and that what interests them is pocketing the bit of cash that will give them a better life.

Annie: It's true; you're right. What is funny is that I've often listened to this program and have always thought that there must be a way to cheat, but I've never thought of this solution.

Marie: It's a solution where you run the risk of passing for a homosexual or a lesbian or a thief or an exhibitionist for about fifteen minutes. It's something to laugh about during the week that you spend the money that you've won! But the people who go there want to show, in the end, that they are a true couple, a traditional couple, in other words, an exceptional couple. People are ashamed to show that they aren't a classic couple or that there are problems within their couple.

Where is love in this story? Where is the game and the pleasure, complicity, all of that which makes people able to live within a couple? All of that flies away when the consecrated image of the couple appears.

If you know a man and a woman who form what we would call a "good couple" and if you tried to understand what binds them together, you would discover each time that these people live outside of the stereotyped image of the couple towards which everything directs us.

Annie: The degree to which you don't mean "couple" when you say "couple" must be stated. When we hear the word couple, we hear the entire ideology which trails along behind it, we hear fidelity, exclusion. . . . For you, this isn't a "couple," and I understand what you mean. It makes me think of a very good work by Camus called *La femme adultère* [The adulterous wife]: a woman who, each night, would leave her husband and go to look at the stars. It's a magnificent work.

Colony, paternalism: two words, Siamese twins, which haunt me, which I encounter at every turn. Is this reality, or is it due to my morbidly obsessive nature? How to know where authenticity begins and where the brainwashing, the abnormal, the cultivated, the domesticated ends? Is it possible that after all of these millennia, a human being can manage to separate the two? Can one keep the core that is the self intact, absolutely solitary, and perfectly free? Can one encounter it outside of dream, and the illogical, the unconscious, the inhuman? I don't know.

I have always compared colonization to the traditional couple and to what it yields: the family. And, just as I don't know a good traditional couple (what we generally call a couple is only, in reality, an association, a scheme, a false front, or a funeral home), I don't know of a good colony.

Why is it that, in my childhood, I felt that colonization was a kind of shame, even though it was presented to me as natural and even sacred? I was on the comfortable side, the side of the colonizers, the side of morality and God. I believed everything that my mother told me. I knew her to be the source of the truth, a fountain of purity, a lake of goodness. Only diamonds, roses, and butterflies could leave her mouth, as in fairy tales. But in the clarity of my childhood, I saw that what she said did not correspond with what she did. I did not find that what she pointed out to me as the good life was, in reality, good. I did not understand anything. To survive this life, I had to close up my eyes, nose, and ears, because what I saw, smelled, and heard was unjust, terribly unjust. I can say that the first fifteen years of my life were torn, plundered by that: the love that I had for my mother, which dragged charity along with the obstinacy of an ant, and the misery of the Arabs who, she said, were a fatality, an incurable ill, a curse.

The first seed of strife was sown by my mother herself during the winter of 1939–40, at Christmas. I was ten.

To celebrate my maturity, my mother decreed that I would help her, this year, with her annual New Year's visit to the shantytowns and poor neighborhoods. I must begin to learn how to be practiced in charity. Because, to be well done, charity demands a number of rites, gestures, words, and mimes which require a long apprenticeship.

A great agitation reigned over this time of year: we emptied out the cupboards and the wardrobes, collecting all of the clothing and the linen that was no longer usable and that the servants of the house didn't want because—this was the least we could do—they had first choice. All of this material was polished, patched, folded, and put into piles with a label above each one: Melkramech family, Benyaya family, Gomez family, etc. During this time, those in the kitchen were hurrying to make fruitcakes, savory cakes, shortbread. It perfumed the entire house. I was in heaven! How good we were at our house! First the poor people and then, once the work was done, we would have ours.

On the big day we piled the presents into large wicker baskets that we somehow or other fit into the car. Under the circumstances, we sat on the front seat, next to my grandmother's chauffeur, Kader. I adored him, and he profited from the situation to put his hat on my head and make me believe that I knew how to drive!

At the last minute, my mother had added to the clothes and cakes already gathered some old toys and wreaths and faded Christmas ornaments from last year. It was a real Christmas, I guess.

I left feeling joy and pride. I knew the poor well and I liked them. The poor people, to me, were the farm workers who lived in low houses arranged around the courtyard and whose children were my best friends during vacation. I was going to meet the poor people of Algiers; perhaps I would make some new friends! I was that stupid when I was young. . . .

It took a long time to get from our neighborhood to the neighborhood where the poor people lived. Finally we arrived in an area of town which I had never seen. A frightening and incomprehensible place. It was called Bobillot City. It was the first city that the HLM, the housing council, had constructed in Algiers.

I had hardly gotten out of the car when I was overtaken by a vague desire to vomit. In front of me, scattered on the side of a bare hill, were tall gray apartment buildings with narrow windows. They stood against the immense sky. Muddy streets led up to them, bordered by round clumps of weedlike grass which grew among the debris of buildings, scrap iron, wheelbarrows without handles, and ladders without rungs, the wreckage of former construction projects.

Kader carried a basket. We walked in front. My mother held my hand and made some last minute recommendations: "Say 'hello' very politely. These are very unhappy people, you know. We must help them even if they are not like us." I had a heavy heart. This place weighed on me; I had never known anything like it. It seemed as if I were entering into the kingdom of unhappiness. My mother appeared at ease and that reassured me.

First, the prison of the staircase, which was stinking, narrow and dark, with cracked steps and walls black with filth. My mother ordered, "Don't touch the banister, and don't put your fingers in your mouth. You'll take a bath when we get home." It was swarming with germs inside, you could almost see them. And when a door opened, they surged toward us at a gallop, mixed with odors of toilets, fried food, and Valda's pastilles, medicated fumigating lozenges. Humble people appeared who took us into hovels full of artificial flowers and posters; often, on the main wall, there was a brilliant tapestry which depicted a tiger wounded by an arrow, dying against a yellow sky amid black palm trees; unless it was an elephant or even, sometimes, a deer. As if it were a litany, we heard: "Thank you, thank you, sarha, sarha. . . ." They knew my mother. She had already helped them, cared for them. She knew the names of everyone in each family and knew all of the sickness they had had during the past year. We left again among "Thank yous" and "sarhas".

For me, this wasn't right. A terrifying thought slowly formed in my mind: "I am not charitable." What a shock! But why? Why was I so confused? Why did I take no pleasure in giving? Why did these poor people make me feel ashamed? Where did this sense of shame come from?

Twenty years later, when I tried to bring myself back to life in a torturous change, these buildings often returned before my closed eyes, sentinels of misery, dreadful, ugly and solid.

In my blind pursuits, my perilous trials and errors, I generally saw them standing there following a white period, when my unconscious would yield nothing and would leave my memory like a blank screen. No images, no words, nothing. Despair: I will never find, I will never be cured. This absence of images and words is the most important obstacle I have ever encountered. I felt as if I had cut my lifeline. I was certain that I had lost the keys to existence and had let them fall into the very vertigo which inevitably spiraled them slowly further and further away from me. I felt that I was lost, given up to the desires, wishes, and angers of others; I felt hunted; I felt worthless. I floundered in this void like a drowning woman flounders in waters which will not buoy her, agitating the void with useless gestures, biting into the water. I did this until the alienated woman's agitation brought gray tinted images to the screen of my memory, invariably bringing a more precise image of Bobillot City to life: "Doctor, I see the cheap housing in Algiers."

These images were heavy; they corrupted and exposed the open grave.

Especially the skeletal woman with her little daughter in her arms, the day of our Christmas visit.

What had been immediately agonizing about this house was its emptiness. There was only one table on a clean tile floor in front of a curtainless window which let in the northern light—cold, bluish, cutting. There I was in my pulled up socks, my good walking shoes, kilt, gray shetland sweater and Scottish beret in front of another little girl, the first child I had seen since we began our depressing visits.

She was a girl who resembled a fetus, with skin the color of skin that has been in the water for a long time. Her arms and legs were folded in upon themselves, and she was curled up on her mother's breast. Her face was sharp and ardent, and she had half hidden it in the housekeeper's apron. That is because, on this side, she was missing an eye. At times, you could see the eyelids sunken into the orbit, behind which there opened a rosy crater.

Trained as I was, I immediately looked away and made as if I had seen nothing. One does not stare at someone else, especially if that person has a defect. But my heart beat and my desire to vomit leaped.

My mother busied herself, sorted her packages, her bits of dead wreath, an old doll that I didn't like, her savory cake. . . . "Thank you! Oh, thank you, Madame!"

"And how old is your little girl?"

"She's eighteen months old, madame."

"And what is her name?"

"Her name's Viviane, like Viviane Romance."

The woman smiled, tried to hold the child out in front of her so that she could be seen. But the child resisted, wanted to keep her head hidden in her mother's neck, with a coquettish air.

"And what is wrong with her little eye, the little rascal?"

"She was born like that, missing an eye. It makes her look like she's winking all the time! We call her our little flirt. We'll make you into a flirt yet, right Viviane?"

Viviane understood that her mother was speaking about her and was saying funny things. She fidgeted and hid her face. She already knew that something was wrong with it.

I was paralyzed, looking at my polished shoes. "Flirt" was a nasty word, one of the words which reached me across the winding streets of language.

Children demonstrate better than any treatise that words live, that they are made of skin and bone, blood and tears, laughter and fear; that they tremble, speak ironically, are mean, dirty or kind; that they are the ambassadors of the tastes, desires, wills, and doubts of each human being. This is what words transmit to children who, what is more, don't know the vital principles behind them. The "be good" of the father and the "be good" of the mother don't have the same meaning. They designate two different goodnesses. The child knows this.

"Flirt", a word of shadow, of something hidden, a word belonging to the wrong. A "flirt" was a woman who winked at men with an unnamable goal, to accomplish an indescribable act. Yet an act which was wholly within my reach, possible. I suspected that the rigorous education of which I was the object was only undertaken so minutely in order to direct me away from committing this act in shame. I must not, at any price, become a "flirt" one day. A "flirt" was disgusting, sordid, dirty.

And yet this woman was saying that her child would be a "flirt," and this made my mother laugh! How was this possible? What was the difference between this child and me? Was money the thing that separated failure and success, shame and honor? Was money a reward? How did we merit it? Our money wasn't seen, no one at home touched it, no one worked. Our money was in the earth, in banks. How was it owned? How does that create ownership?

I didn't understand anything, but I smelled something fishy underneath all of this, something unhealthy. They taught me, "Happy are the poor," "You will earn your bread by the sweat of your brow," "It is as difficult for a rich man to enter the kingdom of heaven as it is for a camel to pass through the eye of a needle." And yet everything else told me that paradise was at my doorstep, while it was off-limits to this poor little girl because she was going to become a "flirt." There was a lie somewhere, some kind of trickery; and for the first time, in confusion and disorder, I dared to doubt my mother and her principles. I understood that I belonged to a class which enjoyed privileges which were, in some way, contestable.

Our journey ended in a household where the children swarmed like mice. Dressed in rags, they beat their arms and legs against the cold of year's end. Their mother explained that she only had enough clothes for half of them, so that they took turns going to school and playing outdoors. She didn't seem to be complaining, really; and that choked me, because to miss a day of class was a major affair for me. I knew that my future as well as my brother's depended in large part on our diligence in our respective classes.

The woman was happy with what we gave her. She said, "This will make a real Christmas Eve celebration with what I've already made," and she proudly led us to a corner where, on a cook stove, a strong-smelling stew simmered. She lifted the cover of the pot and we leaned over to look at a few thin slices of horse meat which were cooking with onions and olives. I found it repugnant. It resembled the dishes we gave to the dogs on the farm.

I had hardly stepped outside when I vomited. My mother diagnosed that I was ravenous and that these visits were very tiring.

From that day forward, I began to consider our electric trains, motor scooters, walking and talking dolls almost as stolen objects. I could no longer feast on turkey and lobster. The others were there, in the village. I guessed that charity could do nothing for them, and that, moreover, my family would do nothing else for them.

Marie: This Christmas so struck me that even today charity, paternalism, demagogy provoke such a sense of disgust and revulsion in me that I want to vomit.

For example, it is impossible for me to employ someone to come and clean my house.

At one point, I did employ someone. I remember that I explained to this woman that she was doing a job which I could not do and did not know how to do; that, consequently, her job was important and she was free to organize it as she wanted to, taking initiatives and responsibilities. But wasn't I practicing the very same demagogy! This woman knew that she was doing the most menial job in the world, and she didn't give a damn about what I was saying. It was a catastrophe. She began to play the housekeeper and I the master. I set out with my great words, I showed her my check stubs, I tried to make her believe in equality. . . . At the end of a week she was pilfering little things from the kitchen, she fibbed about work hours, and I was being charitable by closing my eyes to it all. In a week, all the tics of paternalism had resurfaced within me. I couldn't bear it. I was ashamed of myself.

And yet I recall a woman who came to clean Jean-Pierre's house in Canada. I don't remember why he hired her. He telephoned an agency and a woman arrived in a Chevrolet. In the trunk were all the necessary supplies: broom, electric polisher, vacuum, different cleaners. She stayed for two hours, and when she left the place was impeccable. It was expensive, but I didn't feel as if I had employed a maid. She was a person who accomplished a certain job in a professional manner. Moreover, men do this sort of thing over there.

Annie: Housekeeping is a job unlike any other. I don't think that any form of housework can be simply done. It is always distorted by the fact that it must fall on the woman of the house. It's woman's work. On the one hand, it isn't considered work; on the other hand, a woman who is paid to do another woman's work must think, "I'm doing what she should do. She pushes this off onto me . . .," etc.

A housekeeper's work wouldn't be the same if there were, in all of society, an equal sharing of housework. There are things that I really enjoy doing around the house, but the pleasure I get in doing them is always corrupted by the fact that it's a job that comes back to me, that I must do. It's a trap.

Marie: Women who employ other women as house-

keepers take on a great responsibility and bring a considerable wrong to women's work which is still, in spite of all of the
great oaths spoken and official speeches, an inadequately
paid profession, discredited and inferior. Sometimes, in periods of unemployment such as the one we are experiencing
now, a woman's work is even seen as a caprice, almost as a
wrong against nature, their nature being to stay home and do
work for free. . . . In current demagogy, which tends to give a
sort of nobility to manual labor, we do not put this in terms of
the feminine—that would be to do it a disservice. Yet 50
percent of production work is furnished by women, 75 percent of minimum wage earners are women, women make up
nearly 40 percent of the working population in France, 59
percent of unemployed persons under 25 are women, and 52
percent of those seeking employment are women. The
country's work force is conjugated in the feminine. The
country needs them; and yet there is a 30 to 35 percent
difference in salary between men and women. I took all of
these numbers from the Ministry of Labor and not from an
association of crazed, privileged feminists or from an office of
the opposition.

I was there when Mr. Beullac, the Minister of Labor,
came to speak to some representatives of the French woman's
work force. He had the numbers I just gave you in his hands,
along with many others which were despairing, derisory,
humiliating. He began to speak in a bit of a babyish tone, the
tone that men have made a habit of using with women, old
people, children, and animals: "You can see that I've come—
that I've kept my promises to come, and so you see that you
must have confidence in men; moreover, I am not speaking
about women's work, but about working women. . . ." As if to
say, "I know your little fancies and I make allowances for
them." Then he changed his tone in the face of the audience's
coldness; he was even in a very tight situation, because what
he had to say was that nothing would change for a long time.

He didn't swear it; but that is what we all understood. Immediately after the end of his speech, he was in a hurry to leave, a woman representing a large syndicate caught his sleeve just as he was departing the gallery. She demanded precise details, dates. He was incapable of giving them to her; he could only make vague promises. The woman said, "I doubt it." He answered, "You're wrong. . . ." It was pitiful and discouraging.

Of course, it would have been a better day if the women workers had said, "Thank you, sahra, thank you." But good habits are lost more and more often these days. Our fathers aren't spoiled.

It's fair. It isn't fair. All of my life spent surveying the comings and goings of justice. Gauging, measuring, weighing by hand and by scale, compensating and spending. . . . And there is still water to turn the mill of my mind! Think of it: I am a woman, was born in Algeria into a family of colonists, and I am a writer (that means that I, like my colleagues, sign an unjust contract that was drafted in 1917 and is susceptible to modifications according to the commercial success that each writer obtains. It's what we call bit by bit . . .). And yet I can't complain; there are other women writers who are also Black and Jewish! It isn't a stroke of chance that the nineteenth century French feminists associated their problem with that of Black people.

There is always this impression that I cannot rest, that I must continue to speak, write, witness, and lay claim. The causes of the colonized, of children are always around me like stubborn companions. They are stubborn companions who are demanding as well as powerless, and I cannot refuse them my vitality, my luck, or my big mouth.

It is a joy to see big mouths multiply! The courageous voices of women who came before us and the new voices: bold, intelligent, inventive. It seems to me that grass is beginning to grow in the desert, that speech is becoming less formal, that our true words are beginning to be heard.

I need no more proof of this than the reaction of the CNPF to the statement on the "Problems posed by the working conditions of women." This statement, precisely and seriously completed by the Committee on working women, depends on the Minister of Labor, who is hardly a revolutionary. In other words, I'm using official governmental sources.

I quote from excerpts of the "Observations of the Representatives of the CNPF," published as an appendix to the statement:

> Without in any way calling into question the sincerity of the observations reported under the title, "The Work Environment," or those reported under the title "Professional Maladies," the Representatives of the CNPF felt it necessary to present two observations:
> The first observation concerns the subjective nature of these testimonies.
> . . . .
> The second remark speaks to the fact that the examples are cited in a manner which makes them seem to represent a permanent situation.
> . . . .
> In one of the cited descriptions of a food company, a description was removed of "cockroaches and worms feasting under the chopping blocks."
> . . . .
> In another food establishment, since "Isolex 77" came into use, the irritations have disappeared. Not a single worker had gnawed hands. They were provided with waterproof aprons, double thick rubber boots, and were protected from the ground by plastic gratings.
> [I wonder how "gnawed" they were for the management to have invested so much in their protection. . . .]
> In conclusion, . . . efforts are made either spontaneously or on the intervention of personnel representatives to ameliorate the working environment and conditions, and results are obtained. . . .

I like the words that the editor of the CNPF quoted. They are difficult to hear, and they lay blame more than technical words do because they skim very near the truth. The "worms" and "cockroaches" and "gnawed hands" will move a mountain and disturb hypocritical, official speech.

Hypocrisy consumes us, surrounds us, imprisons us. Especially that of the monstrous fright that is the mother. I really must begin to speak of that!

It is because the working woman is a mother that she is often absent and is, consequently, underpaid and underemployed.

It is because she remains a mother that night work is forbidden to her. It isn't true that women want to exhaust themselves each night. Nobody wants that. But it pays better to work nights, and women want to survive. They have had enough of life's troubles. Of all troubles—just like men! And they know, rightly, that they can better raise children when they do not live in want.

The placement of power in society makes the mother seem as if she is still the mother of the nineteenth century. That is wrong.

To add to the mother, there was the father, a character with a mustache and hat who held out his arm so that the mother could lean against it. He protected the mother. He made sure that the sacrificial gold of his wife was never tarnished. But the father has disappeared. He left to search for money and no longer does anything else. The mother remains alone to uphold the family; and this makes her own blemishes appear: she is only second best, she doesn't know how to speak, her crown is a sham.

The father is lacking in our lives. Man is lacking in our existence. In western, middle-class communities—whether they are royal, common, communist or just plain middle-class—the man is no more than a mocked master and the woman an abused mother. The children suffer to be born of such a couple.

I don't want to plead for these false masters, these men, because I only know how to use words from my inner self and I am not a man. I can only speak of them as a spectator. I see them drive their cars with more or less mastery, see them drink their cocktails at the bar, see them belch and fart in the satisfaction of a job well done. I have seen them make war or fight in the street. I hear them speak in political assemblies and listen to their phrases run one into the next. I know how they return home each evening to be served and loved. I know their desirous glances at young buttocks and breasts that make their flies bulge. I have caressed their sweetness after love. I find their tenderness as precious as diamonds. I like how they smell; I like their large hands. I do not like their pretension, their delusion, their total contempt for anything having to do with women. I pity them when I see them uphold their virility. I find them naive, ignorant, lost, as are sometimes rich people or kings when they suddenly become aware of the vanity of power. I find them stupid, contemptible, and grotesque when they believe in their own superiority because that is the way it is.

I want to talk about the woman, about this abused mother.

I tremble with fear and anger for her.

Mother is a word full to bursting with senses and images—It is ready to explode. It is dangerous. It rumbles all throughout our language: Mother Michel, our sainted mother the church, the mother country, Mother of God, mother of cider, grandmother, Mother Tapcdur, mammy, Mother Superior, adoptive mother, mother office, mother-in-law, dura mater, unmarried mother, unknown mother, big mamma, the mother of the family, the good mother, the joy of motherhood, Mother Goose, the Queen Mother, mother of many children, mother hen, mater dolorosa, mommy, mama, mummy. . . .

Whatever road we follow, we always return to this cell—mother, this perpetually fecund Medusa, this mass of moving and shifting forms which is regularly made to deliver in spasms. This departure and goal! This place where mystery becomes reality, where the invisible becomes visible, where one becomes two, where acuteness animates dullness, where the round and the long are united. The hollow and the point. This beauty. This monstrosity. This incomprehensible thing, half human.

Humanity rests in her belly where the sea shuttle between the water of creatures and the water of gods is found.

The woman carries that. All of it. She carries it like a country wears a flag, and like the Tabernacle carries God. Like scales hold the weight of justice. Like the candle gives light and the guitar plays music. Like the open window makes a breeze in the room . . . without even realizing it. . . .

When the work begins, when the cell is about to divide so that the child can be born, the woman is possessed of a force superior to her which takes command of her body. She cannot direct the contractions which stiffen the muscles of her stomach, their intensity, their frequency. She cannot take a bit of rest.

And when the three or four huge waves of the final expulsion seize her pelvis, when she feels her vagina dilated like a sun, when her opening is blooming like a huge dahlia, she is there, the woman, torn, by whom or by what? She does not know.

Derisory words come to her, the words of beings to which she no longer belongs; they say, "You're as big as an apple," or "You're completely dilated. Push." Before that, it was "small apple," before that "half dollar," and before that "a quarter." This is all that has been found to translate for the woman what she feels but does not see: the words of the market, money, fruit! She herself knows that it isn't a case of burgeoning commerce between her legs; these words are unbearable to her. She brushes them aside with the movement of her head or arm, with a plea, "Leave me alone." Her look is filled with the unspeakable. Leave her! She has life between her legs.

She does not know why it's like that, why her body does that, why it has developed in her, why it's become a child. And it is in this and this alone that she is different from man. All women have this in them, whether or not they have had a child. The youngest girls and the oldest women have it as well.

Does this represent such a power that everything has been done to strangle, to lessen, to minimize, to diminish it? Has it been necessary to transfer this power to some other domain, so that power becomes a capacity and nothing more? The capacity to hold a child? The woman would be nothing more than a container, a barrel, a cask, pint or liter.

How has this translation taken place? By what perverse distillation, by what serpentine path has the woman had to pass in order to become "Mother"? No book gives this history of the mother. There are scattered studies of the matriarchy in British Zambla or in Kamchatka, and other studies on the mothers of Julius Caesar or Louis XIV. But no one has studied the history of the laws, sciences, wars and religions which have fabricated this occidental monster, the Mother. No one has gone to the roots, beyond the law, science, gods, and combats. How was the lot divided? I'm sure that we'd find something very simple, something that speaks about grasses and meat, something like, "You have one child in your belly and another at your breast. You can't come and hunt with me. Stay here and pick huckleberries for dessert and I'll bring back a wild boar for everyone." It isn't that Mrs. Neanderthal didn't know how to hunt; it's that she couldn't do it, constrained as she was by her children. So she stays there, she "sacrifices" the pleasure she would have taken in catching a boar for her children. And for lack of anything better, she "hunts" huckleberries. It becomes her petty specialty. The glory of combat, the humility of the meal. Danger-security.

And power? Power! Man has the power to move about and to kill for the survival of others. And the woman? She has the ability (the ability?) to procreate. Is this power? This masterwork which develops within her, without her knowing why or how?

It is in this sort of power that doubt, ambiguity, fragility, and vagueness reside. The power would more likely be this eternal feminine than it would be something else, this power that isn't controllable, perfectible; this power which may be, after all, nothing more than a capacity. "I have killed the wild boar with my muscles, with weapons that I have built with my wit and knowledge. You have only to bend and gather up your grasses. And your child—what did you use to make it? My sperm and the sexual act that I decided to do with you." How can you respond to that?

End of power, end of equality. Glory be to the muscles of the hunt.

I don't think that it was a logic much more complicated than that which, in the early part of society as we know it, set up the system of humiliation and crushing cleavage. I think that this is simply how this formidable and innate power of the female of the species was distorted, masked, transferred, disguised and weakened.

After that? After that, I don't know the details, the leaps that were made. All of these machinations, this conspiracy, remained in the shadows. We never look at it. I can only imagine the difficulty involved in simultaneously taking all power from the woman and compressing it into this same power, reduced to the capacity to have children. Then, in making this capacity to have children the glory of the woman— the purpose of all her life.

The mother was born of this sham, this failure. The mother: this saint, this tortured miscreant, this slut, this poor woman!

The mother is the most sophisticated, artificial and least natural character in our society. And it is this freak that is at the center of the family, at the foundation of our communities.

Mothers torture women, children, and men. The mask, costume, makeup, and game of the traditional mother are the sacred yokes which drive women to hysteria, despair, and the insanity of possession. It drives them to useless sacrifice, hypocrisy, stupidity, barrenness and to the most narrow obedience to the false traditions which have made the woman what she is.

In order to maintain the fragile equilibrium established by men, women shouldn't have been taught to read and write. Only ignorance will keep them in their place.

The person who instructs herself, who learns, who understands, will not accept this comedy of manners, the enormous mystification which leads women to masquerade as mothers.

It is impossible not to see the enormous role that mothers play in our country's economy and not to recognize simultaneously the incapacity of the country to do without their services or to remunerate them. Cities would not hold. The new concrete apartment buildings would be nothing more than foul hutches in five years time if mothers, like ants, didn't keep them so carefully—waxing, washing, scouring, scrubbing. The fields would only be fallow ground if men didn't find soup on the table, dry clothes, and a warm bed on returning home. Children would die or run wild if mothers weren't there, fixed, welcoming, expertly caring for them, wiping their noses and loving them.

Mothers are indispensable. But it is indispensable that their work is done for free, for in the state's budget distribution, there is not an envelope for them. If there were one, the state such as it is wouldn't survive the puncture. It is, therefore, a political necessity that the mother remain the mother.

In other times, when people—men and women alike—lived in ignorance and slavery, the division of labor was not undertaken more poorly than anything else. It was, all in all, a distribution of misery. The father and mother, equally needy, yoked to equally tiresome and insignificant tasks. That is as long as money wasn't there. As long as money hadn't made of work what it is. As long as that which gave value to work wasn't money.

When money entered into the dance, the slave, paid a few cents, became a worker; the valet was given a few dollars to mend the oversleeves of the clerk or official—titles of nobility mockingly distributed by the bourgeoisie who had just stolen revolution from the masses. Mothers remained at home, with tradition in their arms and archaism in their bellies, with their hands full and their pockets empty. Thus, they learned that their work was worth nothing, that it didn't merit any title of nobility.

In other words, during a recent epoch, in the nineteenth century, because of the industrial revolution and the insatiable attraction of money to men, the life of the mother was totally and definitely devalued.

I know that all of this is greatly simplified and that an in-depth study must be done on the causes of the decline in conditions of a woman's life in today's society. Catholicism has contributed greatly with its monstrous model, the Virgin Mother:

"How can a virgin become pregnant, my child?"

"By the working of the Holy Spirit, Father."

"A very good answer, my child."

"So the Holy Spirit isn't a bird, it's a pig, father."

"Be quiet! You haven't understood a thing! You'll be excommunicated."

"Oh, I've understood everything, and I don't give a damn about being excommunicated. It's a pig because I find it more sane-tly to be stained than to be un-stained."

This foolishness, which makes me giggle—because it doesn't take much to make me laugh—remains for the majority of French women extremely subversive talk, scandalous and of an impermissible boldness. I am authorized to say that not by statistics, scientific studies, and the confirmation of sociologists, ethnologists, "politologists," and all the other assorted "ologists"; I am authorized by the thousands of letters that I receive which portray the Virgin Mary at bay, plundered, maddened, dumbfounded.

Today, mothers do not understand how all the love, pain, devotion, work, and sleepless nights that they give only lead to the parched vexation of housework, to disenchanted and unemployed youth, and to a solitude broken only by dust, canaries, and knickknacks.

As long as she was kept in the household, the mother could maintain the illusion of being an important person. But now that she works out of the house (forty percent of the work force in France), she can no longer keep these illusions. In factories, business, and in management, she discovers the mother's true face: that of a she-ass. A being that naturally has a taste for and habit of sacrifice, menial tasks, and inferior duties; she is a being who is disposable, whose labor isn't paid in pennies—these modern passports to freedom, but in pride— this fraud.

We are worth nothing!

"Mother" is no more than a hollow word, a cabalistic formula to make us remain calm. Here is what I read in volume 215 of *Le Point,* in an article entitled "Milky Delight":

> If you are one of these mammas who has enough milk to feed three babies, play the role of nurse for children to whom mother's milk is indispensable. To do this, you simply contact a "lactarium" in order to give your milk. An infant welfare specialist will come to your home, bringing the necessary material (electric breast pump, sterile bottles) and will explain their use to you. The bottles, which you store in the refrigerator, will be collected every two days. You will be paid $2.40 per liter on a monthly basis.

Not even the price of a mediocre Bordeaux, and on the condition that you have a refrigerator!

It would be interesting to make a comparison to the price of a kilo of sperm (with or without refrigerator).

The mother's body—this so-called sacred vessel—is, in fact, worth nothing. I remember an incident that took place during the Assembly's debates on the issue of abortion; a delegate took the floor to express his displeasure. He explained that the level of the discussion in progress was unacceptably low and that we had reached the lowest possible level when we discussed at length whether abortion should be practiced during the tenth or twelfth week. What possible importance could that have!

I detested this man for his ignorance and for the scorn that he showed for our bodies. These weeks are dreadful. They are thick with our desires, fears, love, and many basic questions: Do I have the right to bring forth a life? Is there life within me? What does it mean, to live?

I wonder what this man would have said if an assembly of women got together to decide if it was better to operate on a man's prostate when it reached the size of a cherry or the size of a tangerine! And yet, their prostate doesn't even imply a question of life.

Truly, the mother no longer means anything, and it is this fact which makes her sick.

Annie: You might say that analysis put you in touch with your body. It seems as if there was a conflict between your mind and your body and analysis reconciled them.

Marie: Certainly, there was a very strong conflict between my body and my mind, and analysis fixed things. But, in spite of analysis, I still sometimes enter into a conflict with my body. It takes a beating. I direct everything inward. From the first worry, difficulty, or contradiction, I get a headache or a cold—anything. Only now I have taken to asking myself, "Why am I sick? Do I have a reason to be sick?" Whereas before I just let myself fall into illness.

I know that my disgust with my body is a product of my childhood. My mother told me that I had large feet and little eyes and that my back was too highly arched. She said all of this to me because, in fact, she thought that I was very pretty and attractive, and she was afraid that I would "abuse" my body. She believed that she could protect me from lust in this way. . . . She told me that later. Or rather, she told me that I mustn't compliment my daughters too much or they would turn into flirts. . . .

When I was little, I subjected my body to very difficult tests—to cold and to hot—and I dressed in the most discreet manner possible. Today I do gymnastics. And I continue to make my body carry my worries.

There was an event that I didn't mention in *Les mots pour le dire* because it was enormous and it might have taken the book in a direction that I didn't want it to go.

It is something that happened when my mother died. I felt this death with extreme intensity.

When I learned of this death, I was seated in front of some editing work that I was doing for a journalist. The telephone rang in the room, but I was absorbed in my work and paid no attention to the conversation. Then the man's hand fell on my shoulder, and his low, rich voice, which had very clear inflections on certain accents, said, "Your mother has just died." I felt the sadness of his words in the pressure of his hand. I also felt the contradiction: this event which meant nothing to him was going to delay our work. I was afraid of losing my job. So, I proved my absolute mastery over the situation (which went well with the staunch virility of the text we were correcting), and calmly said something like, "That is in the nature of things," or, "It was bound to happen," without lifting my eyes from the pages. And we returned to our work.

Letters exploded, words capsized, sentences drew

themselves out like snaky sirens, paragraphs were immense deserts which I could not bring myself to cross.

My mother had lived her final months like a hunted animal seeking refuge. She had found death. Just as well— she could no longer live, she no longer wanted to live.

But all the same, my mother was dead! DEAD! My mother is dead! My mother, this hem in my life's fabric, this limit to my understanding, this borderline of my desires and prison of my madness. This death, eternal absence, stupefying disappearance, was necessary to break the walls, disintegrate the bars, to crumble the barriers which enclosed us in the confines of both hatred and love. I was alone, I was one, unbelievably, unbearably. I was left to this incandescent liberty which burned everywhere around me.

And her refreshing hands on my feverish skin? And her voice when she sang, "Hush Little Baby"? And the soft skin of her checks right next to her ears? Never again! She blossomed with security and gave off the scent of love, like all mothers. Never again? Never again.

And my cradle, her belly, my beginning, her milk, my origin, the light between her thighs? Never again? Never again! All perished? Yes, all perished.

Again, her body, which works, her poor worn out body, swelled by my life, consumed by death!

Release me, I cannot bear this suffering.

And that dangerous sword of hatred between us? And her words which cut me like a whip? And her principles which chiseled my self into a shape suitable to her? And her God who bled for my sins? And her inestimable sacrifices? And the debts that I cannot repay, the enormous bills that she brandished: her time, her youth, her nights, her pleasures, even, perhaps, her talents? An end to all of that. The tally stopped abruptly. Her death made me rich.

Richer and freer than I had ever been.

The letters danced before my eyes—a's, p's, and e's. I

could no longer read. I did poor work. . . . I remembered that during my first year at school, I could not pronounce "gn." The instructor slapped my hands with a ruler because of that. I was ashamed of myself: and if my mother found out? Each "gn" that I saw made me sweat. I had to apply myself, my mother couldn't find out about that fault.

My mother was dead now. I had nothing to fear but myself.

Marie: . . . I was violently affected by my mother's death; it was a terrible storm. I refused to go see her during the visitation, refused to go to the burial, and I refused to go to the cemetery. I thought that all of these pretenses were stupid. She and I had been torn so far apart. One member of my family called to reproach me. I should have come, everyone was there to mourn her except her own daughter. This absence was a blot on "us." There were enough people to leave millions of flowers on her grave.

I decided to break all the ties that held me to these people, whom I only continued to see because my mother existed. With my mother dead, I no longer had anything to do with them.

The months passed and a throbbing guilt shot into my soul: I should have gone to the cemetery.

My mother's death corresponded with the end of my psychoanalysis. I was well, I only went to see the doctor occasionally.

Every year in January, I have a pap smear done to detect uterine cancer. That year, I went to have the smear done as usual. It was a routine that had been a part of my life since I had my first child. Nothing in particular was wrong with me.

The results were positive. They did the same test in another lab, then a biopsy, then a colposcopy. There was no doubt, I had the very beginnings of cancer. It is called a dysplasia with an irregular core.

I was terribly frightened. My children were still very young! The oldest was thirteen!

I phoned my psychoanalyst to tell him that I wanted to see him at the first opportunity and went to his office one evening with all the records of my tests.

He looked at the results very carefully. It took a few moments. I was sitting in front of him—I hadn't stretched out on the couch in months—and watched what he was doing. He closed the records and remained pensive for a moment; then he lifted his eyes toward me and said, "Are you happy?"

This left me dumbfounded. I was ready for anything but that. I had come for him to help me fight my fear, not for him to remove my cancer. Yet in my stupefaction, I understood that this is just what he did. In spite of the seven years of analysis that I had behind me, I had never made the connection between my mother's death, my desire not to see her burial, the guilt that was a product of that desire, and this new cancer which grew in my belly.

Do you know what I did? I began to laugh. Not a hysterical laughter, not at all. Rather, I laughed a soothing laughter, a light laughter which relaxed me and was like a well spring or a bath.

The next day I went to the cemetery, and three days later I went and had my operation, exactly as if I were having a mole removed. I knew that it was nothing more than that.

At the cemetery I cried like a baby. I reconciled myself with her completely, truly, totally, deeply. I dared to swear that I loved her and that I missed her and that we both had lived terrible lives, but that they were so important!

Once more I had internalized, I had brought the unrecognized distress caused by my mother's death into my own body.

Annie: When you began, you said, "I have always been in conflict with my body," as if your mind were in conflict with your body. But both of us know that there isn't a body on one side and a mind on the other. You then spoke of your mother, who was cruel to your body. As if, finally, the mind is what really goes against the body, refuses it, says "no" to the body. When you say that you are fortunate to internalize, perhaps this really means that the conflict doesn't remain an abstraction but becomes something physical. It is something that is internalized because it is the root.

Everything revolving around the cancer which manifested itself in your body at the time of your mother's death is really what is essential. In fact, perhaps it is yet another way of living what she gave to you.

Marie: Yes, that's right. My body is my mother.

Annie: Or the refusal of your mother. Or, "I want more of this mother within me, this mother who struggles against my body, so I'll give myself a cancer."

Marie: I feel as if my body belongs to my mother, or to my parents at the extreme; and I feel that my mind belongs to me. She made my body, I can make my mind.

Annie: Yes, but what is the mind if it isn't the rapport that we have with our bodies? And in your rapport, your mother is there for some reason.

Marie: Yes, but I can act on that—I can change this rapport; whereas I can do nothing with my body—diets, exercise, but nothing major.

Annie: You realize how all of that fits into the order of conflict. You speak about your body as if there were always something within it that belongs to the enemy, something that has to be conquered. You are still combative with it. Your body looks good, it is neither too narrow, nor too constricted, nor sickly. What comes from it and is given to children or to men, for example, is sovereign. But we always feel that it has been won through conflict.

It has always been necessary for you to fight your body, and some of these fights have been perilous. During your hemorrhage, when you were so close to death, you said that you were happy, as if the fight were over.

Marie: Yes, that's true; I liked to think that I would no longer have to bear my body.

I am conscious of this constant combat. It is the motor of my life. I believe that I have always led this life of combat, ever since I was in my mother's womb.

I ask myself what my life would have been like if my mother hadn't said, when I was twelve, that she did everything in her power to miscarry. This avowal was an overwhelming revelation. I felt that I always fought to exist in a world which did not want me. I believe I was late in delivering. I can find no other explanation for the obstinacy that I put into living. Because in other respects, I am a peaceable person, I am not confrontational.

Annie: No, you are not constantly confrontational; you are not an aggressive person, but you are muscular. You are muscular in the same way as a person who has exercised for many years.

Marie: You know that from a certain point in its uterine life, the fetus reacts in its own way to exterior forces. An infant immediately feels the atmosphere and mood of its mother. I believe that I sensed that I wasn't wanted and reacted by fighting. I know what fighting is, but I only know how to fight alone. I don't know how to fight in company. Yet I like to be alone. That is why I like to act—it was a combat with the audience, a fight to make it like me rather than to hurt it.

Writing is combat for me. I write with my body. I sweat heavily when I write.

Annie: In fact, you fight of necessity. If you hadn't, even in your mother's belly, you wouldn't have existed. When you say that you didn't have your period until you were twenty, while you looked like a woman at thirteen, that too is a struggle.

Marie: Perhaps I still wanted to be a child so that she would care for me. I don't know. . . . In any case, it was when

I stopped fighting that I became sick. I put down my fists at one point, accepted being what my mother wanted me to be, and at that time the neurosis began. I can say that from the age of fifteen until I was thirty-six, I was a neutral person, I didn't exist alone. I had to find my violence once more, a violence which had become sluggish, a violence of which I was no longer even aware.

Annie: In fact, your illness was a combat entirely internalized, turned upon yourself. A process of life and death.

Marie: Absolutely.

Annie: Your mother's failed abortion. Your illness which began and materialized with a considerable loss of blood. Isn't all of that finally an abandonment to your mother's desire? You lived your mother's abortion. It's in that way that you died, really.

Marie: Of course. I aborted myself. I no longer wanted myself. I tried to kill myself many times.

Psychoanalysis made me find the paths to myself, and my children brought me into the world. My cure coincided with the end of their childhood, the beginning of their adolescence. I knew too well the havoc my mother brought me without even realizing it; so I was suspicious of my own words and actions. I told my children the truth, whatever risks there were in preconceived principles and laws, and also whatever risks there were in living without them. We decided together that respect was really the only necessary thing. Respect of yourself and of others. We started there and built our family. This doesn't even take into account that they brought me books, music, words, forms, lines which enriched me extraordinarily.

But what an uproar! Everything was overthrown, everything. Even today, I wonder how I tolerated it. It was exhausting. Little by little we learned to know each other. But what an airing out of things! It went from, "Why can't we put our elbows on the table" to, "Why should a mother serve her children," by way of, "Why must the cleaning be done in the morning," for example, or, "What is freedom when we live together. . . ." Together, we became aware that regulation, dirt, and laziness only came during times of uneasiness; we became very aware of ourselves and of others. It was complicated and violent at first; but then the equilibrium which was possible between us came by itself and my life with my children became happy, very happy.

Now they are adults and I don't know what their lives will be like, but I like the paths they've chosen and I think that they are courageous and interesting. We see each other all the time, but we have very sane relationships, no longer mother-child/child-mother. But it is understood that I'm their mother. They know that it is a role I will never refuse to play if one or all of them deem it necessary.

But I am a mother, and I am very distrustful of that person.

You know how my children and I lived for years: the door open, everyone could come in, all of their friends. I told that story in *La clé sur la porte* [The key in the door]. I saw hundreds of young people come and go. Those who came and stayed (sometimes for many months) had problems. And each time, their problem was their mother. Without exception.

What a messy sort of love! For mothers do love their children, and children do love their mothers. But it comes about in total incomprehension and a disregard of one another. I find that troubling. It touches and overwhelms me.

It is difficult to be a mother today. So much work, so much fatigue, so much silence, so many mistakes, so much sacrifice. Why? To find solitude, a husband who remains distant from child rearing. To find a husband who fills the proud shoes of the worker, the begetter, but who has little to say to the person who passes her life and her youth in laundry and dishes and strained budgets, in mending and exhausting errands which require her to run, burdened with baskets of provisions, from work to home. Any mother of a family has transported tons and tons of merchandise in her life, has lifted tons and tons of wet laundry, or pails of water, has held in her arms by the ton the bodies of her babies, of her children.

Mothers are not blind; they see the beautiful women on the billboards, their great figures and long legs, their firm breasts. They know that they have neither the time nor the money to equal that, or even to come close, because beauty is expensive at thirty, forty, fifty. . . .

Mothers are not deaf; they hear the old women at Sunday market and in the neighborhood shops asking the butcher for the heel of the ham and other scraps, asking for spoiled fruit at the fruit vendor, pear cores, and crumbs of biscuits. . . . They have only half of the pension of their dead spouse on which to live!

What kind of perspective do mothers have when they have finished raising their children? Menopause and a rest home.

They don't want that. So they turn inward, they become tough. They clutch what they have and demand their due: presence, love, and respect. They act inappropriately, like people who are afraid. They become possessive, uncompromising, narrow-minded. They hold onto the good old traditions which made a mother into a venerated queen. They don't like the new because the future brings them nothing but abandonment, desertion, and misery.

They make the family a living hell!

Whose fault?

Annie: I believe that what is important is that we are no longer connected to the most fundamental experiences of life, that we don't know how to tie them together to make them into a coherent existence.

Marie: We have lost our contact with everything, even with objects. We have lost our own thread. Especially women. We manipulate matter endlessly, we fashion. What comes from our hands is called a stew or a sweater, hem, cleanliness, order, health, bouquet, whiteness, soup, syrup. . . . These words are empty shells, worthless. What gives them value is no longer in circulation. They no longer have juice or thickness; their true sense is lost. Love, warmth, taste, projects, hope are no longer kneaded into their dough. They no longer contain time, hours, the sun, cold, pain, and patience. They cost money but don't bring a return. They are almost shameful. There are supermarkets and advertisements full of them.

We are barbarizing material and objects and this creates a false sense of life.

We no longer see that cars are like millions of horses whose noise and waste invade our space. We no longer see that the phone is a cohort of messengers who knock furiously at our doors. We no longer see that the sky is swarming with thousands of carrier pigeons which we call planes. We no longer see that our coins and bills are emeralds, diamonds, and golden embossed plates. We no longer know that these objects are the realization of the most insane people, the consecration of the most beautiful dreams. They are no longer matter formed by the spirit. They are no longer any more than products to be bought and sold.

The very form of our material world escapes us; the swift bodies of our cars escape us; the long telephone cord and its handset which links word and hearing, the far away and the nearby, the wings of planes . . . this transcendental life escapes us. . . .

I remember having discovered everything that surrounded me during my analysis. One day it was a fork. I considered it. It had four teeth made especially to poke fairly

firm and large bits of nourishment, four teeth curved in such
a way that they made introduction of that nourishment to my
mouth much easier. And this handle whose flat end was easy
to grasp, why was it so long? . . . So that I don't touch this
matter, so that it doesn't get me dirty. . . . And yet this matter
was matter that I was going to put into my mouth, it was going
to slide into my insides. . . . —So, we can dirty our own
interiors, but not our exteriors?—The fork spoke to me, was
important; it showed me one of the ways in which men think.
It took me to an essential debate between me and myself, for
I found it both useful and hypocritical. . . .

It is this that we have forgotten: the soul of matter, its
qualifications, its cruelty and kindness, its silliness and intelligence, its wisdom and folly.

Women still perceive it, either consciously or unconsciously. But they don't know how or don't dare to say it,
because the roads which lead from matter to words fall into
the gutters of vocabulary, or they pass by so many barriers
and filters that are so efficient that nothing remains of the
living matter when the words come from our mouths. Words
are used more and more often to hide sex and the body. But
the equilibrium between the soul and matter is perfect; it isn't
a question of destroying it. It can destroy us, in the end, and
we aren't far from realizing how this destruction is possible
even now.

Mothers, who have kept contact with matter more
than any other human being, can avoid this destruction if they
can begin to speak freely.

Annie: What we say mustn't serve to send women
running back to their homes, their knitting, their cooking and
housekeeping. Unless of course they are paid to do that. What
must be conceived is a society in which everyone can have a
relationship with objects, matter. . . .

Marie: . . . with the family.

Annie: Not with the family!

Marie: You cannot prevent women from having children, and thus having a family.

Annie: Yes, but they can have it other than how we live as families ourselves.

Marie: Absolutely. I mean to suggest a different kind of family.

Yet another word to open! We have brought out a few! Revolution, couple, writing, matter. And if we took politics!

Annie: And if we dreamed a bit!

Marie: Yes, yes—what do you want to dream of?

Annie: Oh, I want to dream about people. How we want to live, function, what we want to happen, how it would be if it were good!

Postscript by Annie Leclerc

So, here are our thousands and thousands of words, but mostly Marie's, captured, trapped, kept in the now familiar house that is this book. I was going to write "in the *prison* of the book," swept away by the common idea that there is true life and then there are books, certain proof of the real on the one hand and of its disincarnate transcription on the other. I have never thought that a book could be a prison, an enclosure, a death. I know too well its fertile flesh. But a house, yes; it has enclosure, interior, an inevitable fixity. What has been said dwells forever within a house; perhaps even more seriously, what hasn't been said, and what might have been said, and what will never be said all dwell within it too.

So Marie wanted to create a book that wasn't writing, but speech. She wanted the adventure, vagrancy, and the undefinable quality of speech, but also this power unique to speech which makes one say something unexpected and even that which one would never have thought unless she said it aloud. I understood this, agreed with it. Only speech that comes from within me, when the other begins to listen, teaches me what I wanted to know and what I didn't yet know.

We talked, Marie of course, but myself as well; I spoke what came to me from the very heart of her words; we talked a lot, talked and babbled. But when the time came to write the book, Marie found, little by little, in the thread of the offered conversation, the domineering need to write; not to write what had been spoken, but to write these words that speech had touched and awakened, heavy, urgent, and obscure. At the same time, I told Marie of my desire to write a few pages of my own for this book. This book? It was because this book isn't really a book — but is, in some sense — that Marie and I so often went from euphoria to weariness, from gratefulness to anxiety, though not always simultaneously. The lack of clear determination of this enterprise was its charm, but this also created an anxiousness for its future. Very early on I knew that it would be unjust, even false, to incite Marie to come to terms with herself at any higher level. The vague consideration of the things around her or a testimony? The "vague," this vague which is in her soul so strongly, the most vast and immense vague terrain of possibility, audacity, and beginnings; or the "regulated," this regulation which is so necessary to terminate, one time, one day or from time to time the torment of vastness? Speech or writing? In Marie, because of Marie, the one and the other must be given together.

At no price would I eclipse what came from Marie, what was like Marie, or was Marie herself; Marie was an astonishing mixture of the decided and the undecided; she was a person who suddenly began to talk about me rather than about herself, and began to talk about many others, so many others, if not of everyone. Because of Marie, I began to think of things I had never thought of before.

So, at the beginning I said to myself, it's funny all the same, this movement which drives her to writing. Doubtless this movement was the same as analysis; and the word, deployed and abandoned to the tumult of obscurity and confusion, drove her to *Les mots pour le dire,* the writing of an analysis, the inscription of everything but analysis, set out on many levels but certain, dense yet clear, expansive yet focused.

As if writing, even if it is of an entirely different order than speaking, could no longer make due without speech; and as if speech, as we understand and practice it, must from now on be linked to writing to be complete.

Didn't she say to me herself that the book must be, that it be written, in order for the analysis to finally be successful, and that this was the mark of certainty.

I was suddenly surprised to find myself at the heart of another ambiguity that I never had taken the time to examine. Why did I entitle my last book *Parole de femme* [Woman's word] when it obviously merited the title *Ecrit de femme* [Woman's writing]? That had been written, and only written, with the sweat and my body's contractions, insane hope punctuated by despair, all proper to writing.

Speak. Write. No, they truly are not the same.

"This speaks its own meaning": breathe, advance, move, laugh, sing, cry, blurt out, blabber; broken out everywhere from the throat, flower of words, flower in words, to happen. . . .

"It is written": to inscribe knowledge, envisaged by black lights of love, ecstasy, sadness, and the grounds of the destructive proof of the body, shot into the world; of the body other than the passionate body.

But again, "To speak": to touch another, to induce her, smear her, seduce her, to go around her; or the instance where it crushes, forbids, to attack her with words or fire, to bite her or take her away, to repulse her.

But again, "To write": that it is branded in the flesh of reality. That it cannot be forgotten or erased. That the obscure be brought to light, be given.

To speak is to be born; to write is to give birth.

Because I don't believe that our desire to be born stops when we leave our mother's body, nor that our desire to give birth can be realized only in a child. And furthermore, this is not because we haven't yet detached ourselves enough from the mother, or because we were not yet "born" enough in some way, that we so urgently and emotively feel this desire to speak. And it is not in the place of children we no longer have that the urgency to write seizes us.

Each time a discussion or debate begins, somewhere, about feminine creation, or more particularly about feminine writing, a subtle type always appears at one time or another to suggest that we consider creation in general as a substitute for procreation. The last word of this proposition is never far behind, the last word which is, as usual, an invitation to be silent: give these poor men who can't have children the compensatory pride of creation and have children, as you were so admirably and rightly made to do. Why do you need to write?

We write because this must be written. Not only so that the past, childhood, smells, the terrible shock and beauty of first bodies, can achieve their ultimate incarnation in the text. Not only so that the original wounds finally close their great flaps with the thread of written words. But so that what wasn't written is. So that the real is in some way modified, expanded. So that a little new space is given where others will find room to breathe, to grow. To speak.

In making this book which isn't one—but is, in some sense—Marie, undoubtedly without wanting to, allowed me to more clearly envision what I want out of my own books.

That they become transitive books, made only to be crossed. And that other voices find their breath in them, find breath for their own speech.

To dare to say, say everything which isn't said. No longer to whisper in the priest's ear or to confine to the analyst's couch, but to you, all of you, to everyone. There is always someone somewhere who prevents us from saying, a power, dogma, scorn or irony. Marie once told me, on reading my last manuscript, "Sometimes one would think that there is someone outside of your text of whom you have a good picture, someone who menaces you, who somehow makes you afraid. It isn't necessary; you don't need it. Only say what you have to say. Because it is this that counts, that does some good."

Of course, she's right. Absolutely right. But while we still speak, we must also write, opening up new worlds, immodest, indecent, impertinent, so that we can finally speak without having turned our language inside out before hand. One day we must be able to say what we must say to our mothers, lovers, fathers, princes, as well as to our brothers and sisters; just to say what we must say to them as it comes to us. And that is still so far away. The fear inside us, the fear to say, when will it ever be uprooted? And it must happen. We must say. Because we must live for the truth.

From Marie, who went to the very depths of fear and came back strong, joyous, shameless, I learn that fear prowls within me still; but it is enough for me to learn this to feel suddenly unburdened of some black, obscure worry, laughing, fresh, beginning. . . .

And so I must speak about the story of the *wall*. Because this was the day that I began to love Marie. Because it is from this day onward that we began to be friends; but also, it was the day that we stopped talking solely with a mind to this book; and finally because it is because of this story of the wall that I, too, wanted to write a part of this book.

The wall, of course, is a part of these stories, always the most intense and troubling, which as if by chance escaped the recorder either because Marie deliberately pushed the pause button, or because she had forgotten—she said not intentionally-to push the record button. This is how we hear about the terrible and unforgettable discovery by the little rich girl, one Christmas Eve, of the Casabah, where her mother took her to present the poor with a few sweets or used clothes. This is how we hear about the disarray and the distress and the dull, weighty solitude of the day that she took *Les mots pour le dire* to the editor. This day where everything was regulated (this is her word); the agony, analysis, fever, and profound pain of words, the manuscript. And again, the story that we afterward called the math story where she told me—and I remember this being a particularly sunny morning, we were laughing—how much she liked math when she was in high school. It is extraordinary how well I understood her that morning, as I myself remembered. Discreetly, in a corner of her own, as the others of her sex and age were sunk in reading Pearl Buck or Rosamond Lehmann or Colette, she took out a math book and invented increasingly subtle equations. A free space, open to unlimited possible combinations. Rules, finally, which weren't about decency, constraint, enclosure, but were those of a sovereign and innocent game. The pleasure of understanding, of dancing and advancing, of discovery and linking, adjusting, constructing, inventing. Pleasure truly touched by grace, without sin, shame or scorn. Ah well, no. There, too, still, perhaps above all, they wanted her to be ashamed, to feel guilty. She said after graduation: I want to study math. What? That's not feminine, not appropriate. You don't become a well-off, patriarchal, and distinguished colonist, only to have daughters who study math. Marie's indecency doesn't date from yesterday. But they said to her, Logic, for example, isn't very far from math, is it? You should do philosophy. It's almost the same; and more feminine, all the same. So she did philosophy to learn unwillingly that it meant nothing. End of liberty, grace, and possibilities. With math, she did not have to answer to anyone. Only in math. In math, no master, no incarnate authority. In math, no voice to command.

Philosophy is a reign of terror—certainly a sweet terror, but one that changes nothing—and of irony—tough, noncompassionate. (But I really am going to explain this story of the wall; I seem to have forgotten, but I haven't.)

Adorable, anonymous mathematicians, melted, vanished in their product to the point that math is offered to me like the blue sky, the ocean, the ocean which belongs to me as well as to many others because it is nobody's, nobody's. Offered to the point that it is me myself who makes it, even if I am short and awkward. It is enough that I practice to be a little amateur mathematician, serious and amused. I am good at it. No one asks me to explain. My math professor doesn't strike fear in me, even if I make a mistake in my equation, even if he yells at me and gives me a bad grade. It's simply that he knows more than me, that he's used to it. When I grow up . . . me, too, if I want . . . it isn't difficult.

But my philosophy professor . . . philosophers. . . . What is this haughtiness, this distance, this menace? I never am and never will be a philosopher. I learn that I am a nonphilosopher under the philosophical eye.

Mathematical truth never presents itself thus, from the exterior, from on high, because it only exists in that it is invented or discovered by me. Inasmuch as it isn't evidence of my own, it is nothing. Because it can never impose upon me, it will not alienate me.

And it is another sort of truth which is marked in you, from outside, branded in flesh, intransgressible law. And you, you become alienated.

So that when, later, Marie spoke to me of this wall, I felt that there was something terrible which meant, for me, that I didn't know enough, that I hadn't wanted to know.

So, one day, to explain what craziness and alienation are (you employ these terms differently), to explain to me what seems so far away, you suddenly and brutally evoke the time when you saw, from the window of the bus, an inscription on a huge white wall, incised, incisive, THIS IS A BLANK WALL . . .; it was as if this was the hardest, most incompassionate time of your dark confusion: THIS IS A BLANK WALL . . .

For an instant, I saw your face entirely naked. And in this sudden nudity, I saw myself. Doubtless, I only met you with a face that was stupefied, where the sadness awakened in you seemed to struggle. You added, poor, poor wall. . . .

I am a blank wall on which THIS IS A BLANK WALL is inscribed; thus, I am not a blank wall; but I mustn't need the inscription, indelible, it needs me of course. I am and am not a blank wall. What this atrocious inscription denies me is the right to exist.

Compared to this irony, Socratic irony is a game, a trial, a ruse. But perhaps it was this irony, before, and they were right in killing it. . . .

I don't speak of Marie, on Marie; I speak about myself, from myself, from an obscure point that Marie opened up in me when she spoke of herself. Aside from, but I want to say at the heart of, these anecdotes, paths and precipices so distinct to our lives, what needs to be said the most imperiously is that you are me, and I am others as well.

Who hasn't had, one day, a moment of fear of childhood, shame of adolescence, this unmade face, this look of a drowning man capsized by his own troubles. This is the look which Marie evokes in the story of the wall. . . . Every day in the thousands and thousands of schools, a teacher finds fault with a child, comes toward him with a silent and fixed gaze; and the child, oh my love, oh my inconsolable love, raises a face etched with panic, unfathomable panic where all my being is petrified. Every day at the station at Montparnasse, police question a North African, calmly surround him and ask him for his papers; and he who has committed no wrong but that of feeling miserable—this is inexcusable—raises, but more likely retracts this face exactly, exactly this face; and every day an accused man facing his judges, a girl before a man, a sick person before his doctor, a student before his examiner, a man they are going to kill. . . . Because Marie didn't forget, didn't want to forget, I remember. Infinite trembling and immobility, the petrifaction of the bird that is going to be caught.

A child deserted by its mother. A child that is scolded by its father, the bigger and braver scold. . . .

This child is at the heart of me, at the heart of you, at the heart of everyone: I consoled, bantered, flattered, and cured it as much as I could. But I feel that its fear, its personal fear of the master who knows, of the master who judges, will never entirely cease beating its wings.

Someone who knows—someone who pretends to know so that I believe he does—appeals to this fear. When the truth comes from somewhere else, from above, to imperiously engrave itself within me, I am paralyzed by it, seduced entirely by it, ALIENATED. . . . The philosophical regard no longer wants to see a child's fear and trembling, but it is upon this fear that philosophy's power is constituted.

During analysis, isn't the analyst behind the patient, analyzing him, if you will (it doesn't bother me to say "the alienated patient," seeing as how we are all, of course, alienated at the very depths of our childhood trials, in our very own homes); why behind? Who is this person who mustn't, who doesn't know how to see the other? The analyst will hear everything that can be spoken, but the face, the look, when in the absolute nudity of a nightmare the voice doesn't make a sound, sound is cut off, the body broken, ruined, crushed, this look, this very look, will not be seen. Because this, which is the only thing worth seeing, cannot be seen without opening the arms, without beginning to sob, without calling for mother, without this memory of the panic at the center of himself and the panic of one who has never ceased asking for mercy.

Your face, your look, you give these to me full face; but they already were no longer yours. It was us, there where we were together, there where we are together, all of us more or less; us as girls, adolescents, women. More than others, there is this child within us, still so weak, still so fragile, and perhaps forever inconsolable. And then, tell me how it can be consoled when every day in thousands of schools, and in thousands of homes. . . .

When will this evil stop, when will this evil which sometimes even brings death stop?

But we are not dead. Under the inscription which denies it, I hear and you hear the soft plea, the insinuating plea of the wall which lives, which wants, which demands in a low voice an open space, the room to live.

Speak. We must speak. Strong, quickly, however. We must wander, dare the vague, breathe in to the limits of our lungs, breed multiples, indefinite, float, meander, undefine our vast bodies, permit their generosity.

We pull forward, we steal. . . . THIEVES! The voice which comes from elsewhere, from above, judges and misjudges us, suddenly seizes us, freezes us, wrings our throats and petrifies our limbs.

So we must. We must write. Trace our own text, day after day, in letters of blood, of light, of love. Subvert, day after day, the other text that prevents us. So that, day after day, we mine it, sap it, we force it little by little to decay.

One day, I promise you, we will be vague. One day, perhaps, no one, not any child, will ever have this face, this look, again. . . .

SELECT BIBLIOGRAPHY

PUBLICATIONS BY MARIE CARDINAL

Mouchette. Video recording of 1967 motion picture directed by Robert Bresson. Neuilly-Sur-France: Argos Films; Chicago, IL: Facets Multimedia.

Mao (with Lucien Bodard). Paris: Gallimard, 1970.

La clé sur la porte. Paris: Grasset, 1972.

Les mots pour le dire. Paris: Grasset, 1975.

Autrement dit. Paris: Grasset, 1977.

Une vie pour deux. Paris: Grasset, 1978.

Cet été-la. Paris: Nouvelles Editions Oswald, 1979.

Au pays de mes racines. Paris: Grasset, 1980. (Includes *Au pays de Moussia* by Bénédicte Ronfard.)

Le passé empiété. Paris: Grasset, 1983.

The Words to Say It. English translation by Pat Goodheart of *Les mots pour le dire.* Preface and Afterword by Bruno Bettelheim. Cambridge, MA: Van Vactor & Goodheart, 1983.

Les grands désordres. Paris: Grasset, 1987.

Comme si de rien n'était. Paris: Grasset, 1990.

Devotion and Disorder. English translation by Karin Montin of *Les grands désordres.* London: The Women's Press, 1991.

Les jeudis de Charles et Lula. Paris: Grasset, 1993.

PUBLICATIONS ABOUT MARIE CARDINAL

Angellors, Christina. "Den goda och den onda Modern: Om kvinnoidentitet I Marie Cardinals forfattarskap." *Edda: Nordisk Tidsskrift for Litteraturforskning/Scandinavion Journal of Literary Research* 4 (1985): 249–53.

Aubenas, Jacqueline. "Marie Cardinal ou la littérature cardinale." *Revue Nouvelle* 63, no. 2 (February 1976): 228–31.

Baroche, Christiane. "Au féminin." *Quinzaine Littéraire* 281 (16–30 June 1978): 7.

Bourassa, André-G. "Le théâtre: Médéé. Légende du Caucase ou du Québec: La Médéé d'Euripide de Marie Cardinal." *Lettres Québécoises* 44 (Winter 1986/87): 50.

Burguet, Frantz-André. "Marie Cardinal: Une vie pour deux." *Magazine Littéraire* 138 (June 1978): 28.

Cairns, Lucille. *Marie Cardinal: Motherhood and Creativity.* Glasgow: University of Glasgow, French and German Publications, 1992.

———. "Passion and Paranoia: Power Structures and the Representation of Men in the Writings of Marie Cardinal." *French Studies* 46 (July 1992): 280–95.

———. "Roots and Alienation in Marie Cardinal's *Au pays de mes racines.*" *Forum for Modern Language Studies* 29, no. 4 (October 1993): 346–58.

Cesbron, Georges. "Ecritures au féminin: Propositions de lecture pour quatre livres de femme." *Degré Second: Studies in French Literature* 4 (July 1980): 95–119.

Chalon, Jean. "L'enfer selon Marie Cardinal." *Figaro,* 18 September 1987, p. 36.

Dammann, Hiltrud. *Marie Cardinals Les mots pour le dire: Autobiographisches weibliches Schreiben im Kontext der 68er Bewegung.* Heidelberg: C. Winter, 1994.

Daverdin-Liaroutzos, Chantal. "Marie Cardinal: *Les grands désordres.*" *Magazine Littéraire* 246 (October 1987): 74–75.

Donadev, Anne. "Répétition, maternité et transgression dans trois oeuvres de Marie Cardinal." *The French Review: Journal of the American Association of Teachers of French* 65, no. 4 (March 1992): 567–77.

Durham, Carolyn A. *The Contexture of Feminism: Marie Cardinal and Multicultural Literacy.* Urbana: University of Illinois Press, 1992.

———. "Patterns of Influence: Simone de Beauvoir and Marie Cardinal." *The French Review: Journal of the American Association of Teachers of French* 60, no. 3 (February 1987): 341–48.

———. "Subversive Stitch: Female Craft, Culture and Ecriture." *Women's Studies* 17, no. 3 (1990): 341–59.

Elliot, Patricia. "In the Eye of Abjection: Marie Cardinal's *The Words to Say It.*" *Mosaic: A Journal for the Interdisciplinary Study of Literature* 20, no. 4 (Fall 1987): 71–81.

Eriksson, Olaf. *La suppléance verbale en français moderne.* Göteborg: Acta Universitatis Gothoburgensis, 1985.

Glastonbury, Marion. Review of *The Words to Say It. New Statesman* 107 (13 April 1984): 26–27.

Haigh, Samantha. "Between Irigaray and Cardinal: Reinventing Maternal Genealogies." *Modern Language Review* 89 (January 1994): 61–70.

Halimi, Gisèle. *La cause des femmes.* Propos recueillis par Marie Cardinal. Paris: Grasset, 1973.

Hall, Colette T. "'She' Is Me More Than 'I': Writing and the Search for Identity in the Works of Marie Cardinal." Pages 57–71 in *Redefining Autobiography in Twentieth-Century Women's Fiction: An Essay Collection,* ed. Colette T. Hall, Janice Morgan, and Carol L. Snyder, with a Foreword by Molly Hite. New York: Garland, 1991.

———. "L'écriture féminine and the Search for the Mother in the Works of Violette Leduc and Marie Cardinal." Pages 231–38 in *Women in French Literature,* ed. Michel Guggenheim, with a Foreword by Henri Peyre. Saratoga, CA: Anima Libri, 1988.

Labat, Joseph. "Marie Cardinal: *Le passé empiété.*" *French Review* 58, no. 6 (May 1985): 912–13.

Le Clézio, Marguerite. "Marie Cardinal: *Les grands désordres.*" *French Review* 61, no. 6 (May 1988): 987.

———. "Mother and Motherland: The Daughter's Quest for Origins." *Stanford French Review* 5, no. 3 (Winter 1981): 381–89.

Leybold, Fred. "Gide et la petite Marie." *Bulletin des Amis d'André Gide* 52 (October 1981): 549–50.

Lionnet, Françoise. "Marie Cardinal (9 March 1929–)." In *French Novelists since 1960,* ed. Catherine Savage Brosman. Detroit: Gale Research, a Bruccoli Clark Layman book, n.d.

Martin, Elaine. "Mother, Madness, and the Middle Class in *The Bell Jar* and *Les mots pour le dire.*" *The French-American Review* 5, no. 1 (Spring 1981): 24–47.

Minh-ha, Trinh T. "L'inécriture: Féminisme et littérature." *French Forum* 8, no. 1 (January 1993): 45–63.

Powrie, Phil. "Reading for Pleasure: Marie Cardinal's *Les mots pour le dire* and the Text as (Re)play of Oedipal Configurations." Pages 163–76 in *Contemporary French Fiction by Women: Feminist Perspectives,* ed. Margaret Atack and Phil Powrie. Manchester: Manchester University Press, 1990.

———. "A Womb of One's Own: The Metaphor of the Womb-Room as a Reading-Effect in Texts by Contemporary French Women Writers." *Paragraph: A Journal of Modern Critical Theory* 12, no. 3 (November 1989): 197–213.

Reinton, Ragnhild E. "Et liv for to: Marie Cardinals nyeste roman." *Vinduet* 36, no. 2 (1982): 14–16.

Rivière, Anne, and Xavière Gauthier. "Des femmes et leures oeuvres." *Magazine Littéraire* 180 (January 1982): 36–41.

Royer, Jean. "Marie Cardinal: Pour une autre humanité." Pages 57–
    63 in *Ecrivains Contemporains. Entretiens I: 1976–1979.*
    Montreal: L'Hexagone, n.d.
Yalom, Marilyn. "They Remember *Maman:* Attachment and Separa-
    tion in Leduc, de Beauvoir, Sand, and Cardinal." *Essays in Litera-
    ture* 8, no. 1 (Spring 1981): 73–90.

Marie Cardinal, French feminist author of numerous works, has had two novels translated into English—*The Words to Say It* and *Devotion and Disorder.*

ANNIE LECLERC is author of *Origines, Parole de Femme,* and *Pont du Nord.*

AMY COOPER has translated and published excerpts from Charles Baudelaire's *La Fanfarlo* and has published her own poetry in *Resourceful Woman.*

CAROLYN A. DURHAM, Inez K. Gaylord Professor of French and Coordinator of Women's Studies at the College of Wooster, is author of *The Contexture of Feminism: Marie Cardinal and Multicultural Literacy.*